Credits

Author

Anghel Leonard

Reviewer

Edem Morny

Acquisition Editor

Sarah Cullington

Technical Editor

Azharuddin Sheikh

Indexer

Monica Ajmera Mehta

Production Coordinator

Shantanu Zagade

Cover Work

Shantanu Zagade

About the Author

Anghel Leonard is a senior Java developer with more than 12 years of experience in Java SE, Java EE, and the related frameworks. He has written and published more than 20 articles and 100 tips and tricks about Java technology. Also, he has written two books about XML and Java (one for beginners and one for advanced users) and another book for Packt Publishing, named *JBoss Tools 3 Developer Guide*. In this time, he has developed web applications using the latest technologies out in the market. In the past two years, he has focused on developing RIA projects for GIS fields. He is interested in bringing as much desktop to the Web as possible; as a result GIS applications present a real challenge to him.

I would like to thank my family, especially, my wife!

JSF 2.0 Cookbook: LITE

Converters, Validators, and Security

Anghel Leonard

BIRMINGHAM - MUMBAI

JSF 2.0 Cookbook: LITE

First published: April 2011

Production Reference: 1190411

Published by Packt Publishing Ltd.
32 Lincoln Road
Olton
Birmingham, B27 6PA, UK.

ISBN 978-1-849691-62-8

www.packtpub.com

Cover Image by Prasad Hamine (hamine_p@hotmail.com)

About the Reviewer

Edem Morny has been involved in enterprise Java technologies since he got introduced to Java in 2005, using tools and technologies encompassing both the standard JavaEE stack and non-standard ones such as JBoss Seam, Hibernate, and Spring. His experience with JSF includes working with plain JSF, RichFaces, JBoss Seam, and Spring Web Flow's SpringFaces.

He has been an active promoter of Java EE, speaking at workshops and seminars of a national scale in Ghana.

He is a Senior Developer at the Application Development Center in Accra, Ghana, for an international biometric security solutions company, which is leading the development of Biocryptic Identity Management Systems for the global market.

Edem was a technical reviewer for *JBoss Tools 3 Developer Guide* and *JBoss AS 5 Development* both published by Packt Publishing. You'll find him blogging at `http://edemmorny.wordpress.com`.

Table of Contents

Preface

This book will cover all the important aspects involved in developing JSF applications. It provides clear instructions for getting the most out of JSF and offers many exercises to build impressive desktop-style interfaces for your web applications. You will learn to develop JSF applications starting with simple recipes and gradually moving on to complex recipes.

We start off with the simple concepts of converters, validators, and file management. We then work our way through various resources such as CSS, JavaScript, and images to improve your web applications. You will learn to build simple and complex custom components to suit your needs. Next, you get to exploit AJAX as well as implement internationalization and localization for your JSF applications. We then look into ensuring security for your applications and performing testing of your applications. You also get to learn all about Facelets and explore the newest JSF 2.0 features. Finally, you get to learn a few integrations such as JSTL with JSF, Spring with JSF, and Hibernate with JSF. All these concepts are presented in the form of easy-to-follow recipes.

Each chapter discusses separate types of recipes and they are presented with an increasing level of complexity from simple to advanced. All of these recipes can be used with JSF 1.2 as well as JSF 2.0.

This LITE Cookbook gathers together essential recipes for data conversion, validation, and security in JSF 2.0. The recipes are selected from the full length JSF 2.0 Cookbook to provide information and instruction most useful for building and processing forms in JSF.

This book is a LITE edition of a longer book, JSF 2.0 Cookbook. The full edition provides Over 100 simple, but incredibly effective recipes for taking control of your JSF applications.

To find out more about upgrading to the full edition, visit www.packtpub.com/liteupgrade and log into your account for offers and help. If you don't have an account on PacktPub.com, visit today and set one up!

What this book covers

Chapter 1, Using Standard and Custom Converters in JSF covers the standard and custom converters in JSF. We start with implicit and explicit conversion examples, then move on to creating and using custom converters, and we end up with client-side converters using MyFaces Trinidad.

Chapter 2, Using Standard and Custom Validators in JSF continues with standard and custom validators. We see how to use a standard validator, how to create and use custom validators, and how to use RichFaces and Apache MyFaces validators. We also present the new JSF 2.0 validators, such as `f:validateRegex` and `f:validateRequired`.

Chapter 3, Security covers some security issues. You will see how to use the JSF Security project without JAAS Roles, use secured managed beans with JSF Security, and use Acegi/Spring security in JSF applications.

What you need for this book

For performing the recipes from this book you will need the following technologies:

- JSF 2.0 (or 1.2)
- NetBeans 6.8
- GlassFish v3

Also, depending on the recipe, you may also need one of the following technologies:

- Acegi Spring
- Apache Maven
- Apache MyFaces Commons
- Apache Tomahawk
- Apache Tomahawk Sandbox
- Apache Trinidad
- Dojo
- Dynamic Faces
- j4j
- JSF ID Generator
- JSF Security
- JSFUnit
- Mojarra Scales
- Pretty Faces
- PrimeFaces
- RichFaces
- rss4jsf

Who this book is for

JSF developers who want to work with validators, converters and security features of JSF. You don't need any prior knowledge of JSF to use these recipes

Conventions

In this book, you will find a number of styles of text that distinguish between different kinds of information. Here are some examples of these styles, and an explanation of their meaning.

Code words in text are shown as follows: "Validation can be performed only on `UIInput` components or components whose classes extend `UIInput`."

A block of code is set as follows:

```
</h:inputText>
  <h:message showSummary="true" showDetail="false" for="userNameID"
            style="color: red; text-decoration:overline"/>
  <br />
```

When we wish to draw your attention to a particular part of a code block, the relevant lines or items are set in bold:

```
<h:inputText id="userNameID" required="true"
            value="#{userBean.firstName}">
  <f:validateLength minimum="5" maximum="25" />
</h:inputText>
```

Any command-line input or output is written as follows:

```
SET PATH = "C:\Packt\JSFKit\apache-maven-2.2.1\bin"
```

New terms and **important words** are shown in bold. Words that you see on the screen, in menus or dialog boxes for example, appear in the text like this: "When you get the **BUILD SUCCESSFUL** message, you should find a JAR file".

 Warnings or important notes appear in a box like this.

 Tips and tricks appear like this.

Reader feedback

Feedback from our readers is always welcome. Let us know what you think about this book—what you liked or may have disliked. Reader feedback is important for us to develop titles that you really get the most out of.

To send us general feedback, simply send an e-mail to feedback@packtpub.com, and mention the book title via the subject of your message.

If there is a book that you need and would like to see us publish, please send us a note in the **SUGGEST A TITLE** form on www.packtpub.com or e-mail suggest@packtpub.com.

If there is a topic that you have expertise in and you are interested in either writing or contributing to a book on, see our author guide on www.packtpub.com/authors.

Customer support

Now that you are the proud owner of a Packt book, we have a number of things to help you to get the most from your purchase.

Downloading the example code for the book

You can download the example code files for all Packt books you have purchased from your account at http://www.PacktPub.com. If you purchased this book elsewhere, you can visit http://www.PacktPub. com/support and register to have the files e-mailed directly to you.

Errata

Although we have taken every care to ensure the accuracy of our content, mistakes do happen. If you find a mistake in one of our books—maybe a mistake in the text or the code—we would be grateful if you would report this to us. By doing so, you can save other readers from frustration and help us improve subsequent versions of this book. If you find any errata, please report them by visiting http://www.packtpub.com/support, selecting your book, clicking on the **let us know** link, and entering the details of your errata. Once your errata are verified, your submission will be accepted and the errata will be uploaded on our website, or added to any list of existing errata, under the Errata section of that title. Any existing errata can be viewed by selecting your title from http://www.packtpub.com/support.

Piracy

Piracy of copyright material on the Internet is an ongoing problem across all media. At Packt, we take the protection of our copyright and licenses very seriously. If you come across any illegal copies of our works, in any form, on the Internet, please provide us with the location address or website name immediately so that we can pursue a remedy.

Please contact us at copyright@packtpub.com with a link to the suspected pirated material.

We appreciate your help in protecting our authors, and our ability to bring you valuable content.

Questions

You can contact us at questions@packtpub.com if you are having a problem with any aspect of the book, and we will do our best to address it.

1
Using Standard and Custom Converters in JSF

In this chapter, we will cover:

- ▸ Working with implicit and explicit conversions
- ▸ Standard converters for numbers
- ▸ Standard converters for date and time
- ▸ Converters and NULL values
- ▸ Creating and using a custom converter
- ▸ Using converters for `h:selectOneMenu`
- ▸ Binding converters to backing bean properties
- ▸ RichFaces and standard converters
- ▸ RichFaces and custom converters
- ▸ Instance variables in converters
- ▸ Client-side converters with MyFaces Trinidad

Introduction

Data conversion is the process of converting/transforming one data type into another. Before going further and analyzing some aspects of JSF converters, let's see what they actually are and what they are good for.

For this, let's take an example of a web application in which the user has to fill up a simple form with some information, such as name, age, and date of birth. The server component of our application will receive this information as strings, even if we know that they are a string (the name), an integer (the age), and a date (the date of birth). This is the phase when JSF converters enter into the scene and convert the user input according to application requirements. If the submitted information is not successfully converted then the form is redisplayed (this time an attention message is also displayed) and the user can refill the form. The case repeats until the submitted information is successfully converted to the correct type.

In addition, you should know that JSF provides a set of standard converters (used for the most common conversions) and the possibility to define your own converters, known as custom converters (this kind of converters are very useful when the standard converters can't accomplish the desired conversions). Speaking of standard converters, the following are the most used converters:

Converter IDs	Converter class
javax.faces.Byte	javax.faces.convert.ByteConverter
javax.faces.Float	javax.faces.convert.FloatConverter
javax.faces.BigInteger	javax.faces.convert.BigIntegerConverter
javax.faces.BigDecimal	javax.faces.convert.BigDecimalConverter
javax.faces.Character	javax.faces.convert.CharacterConverter
javax.faces.DateTime	javax.faces.convert.DateTimeConverter
javax.faces.Boolean	javax.faces.convert.BooleanConverter
javax.faces.Double	javax.faces.convert.DoubleConverter
javax.faces.Long	javax.faces.convert.LongConverter
javax.faces.Short	javax.faces.convert.ShortConverter
javax.faces.Integer	javax.faces.convert.IntegerConverter

Some JSF tags that support converters are as follows:

- `<h:outputText>`
- `<h:outputLink>`
- `<h:selectManyListbox>`
- `<h:selectMaynyMenu>`
- `<h:inputTextarea>`

- `<h:inputHidden>`
- `<h:outputLabel>`
- `<h:inputText>`
- `<h:inputSecret>`
- `<h:selectBooleanCheckbox>`
- `<h:selectOneRadio>`
- `<h:selectOneListbox>`
- `<h:outputFormat>`
- `<h:selectOneMenu>`

Speaking about a converter lifecycle, you should focus on two main phases named: `Apply Request Values Phase` and `Render Response Phase`. For example, if we assume a form that is submitted with a set of values, a converter for those values, a corresponding backing bean, and a render page, then the application lifecycle will be like this (notice when and where the converter is involved!):

- `Restore View Phase`: The backing bean is created and the components are stored into the `UIViewRoot`.
- `Apply Request Values Phase`: The submitted values are decoded and set in the corresponding components in `UIViewRoot`.
- `Process Validations Phase`: The converter `getAsObject` method receives the submitted values (eventually a potential validator is also called).
- `Update Model Values Phase`: The converted (validated) values are set in the backing bean.
- `Invoke Application Phase`: The phase responsible for form processing.
- `Render Response Phase`: The values that should be displayed are extracted from a backing bean. The `getAsString` method of the converter receives these values before rendering. The conversion results are redirected to the result page.

Using the proper converter is the developer's choice. The developer is also responsible for customizing the error messages displayed when the conversion fails. When the standard converters don't satisfy the application needs, the developer can write a custom converter as you will see in our recipes.

Notice that our recipes make use of JSF 2.0 features, such as annotation, new navigation style, and no `faces-config.xml` file. Especially you must notice the new `@FacesConverter` annotation for indicating to a normal class that it is a JSF 2.0 converter.

Let's start with a simple recipe about working with implicit and explicit conversions.

Working with implicit and explicit conversions

By implicit conversions, we understand all the conversions that JSF will accomplish automatically, without the presence of an explicit converter (in other words, if you don't specify a converter, JSF will pick one for you). Actually, JSF uses implicit conversion when you map a component's value to a managed bean property of a Java primitive type or of `BigInteger` and `BigDecimal` objects.

In this recipe, we will see an example of an implicit and an explicit conversion. Anyway, don't forget that explicit conversion provides greater control over the conversion.

Getting ready

We developed this recipe with NetBeans 6.8, JSF 2.0, and GlassFish v3. The JSF 2.0 classes were obtained from the NetBeans JSF 2.0 bundled library.

How to do it...

Our recipe is based on an imaginary situation where the user should insert their age into a simple JSF form consisting of a text field and a submit button. The submitted age will be implicitly converted and displayed on another simple JSF page. The following is the JSF form (the highlighted code maps the text field's value to the `userAge` managed bean property of a Java `integer` type):

```
<h:form id="AgeForm">
    <h:inputText id="userAgeID" required="true"
                 value="#{userBean.userAge}">
    </h:inputText>
    <h:message showSummary="true"
               showDetail="false" for="userAgeID"
               style="color: red; text-decoration:overline"/>
    <br />
    <h:commandButton id="submit" action="response?faces-
                     redirect=true" value="Submit Age"/>
</h:form>
```

The preceding code snippet makes uses of the new JSF 2 implicit navigation style. The `{page_name}?faces-redirect=true` request parameter indicates to JSF to navigate to the `{page_name}`.

The userAge is mapped into a managed bean as shown next:

```
package users;
import javax.faces.bean.ManagedBean;
import javax.faces.bean.SessionScoped;
@ManagedBean
@SessionScoped
public class UserBean {
    private int userAge;
    public int getUserAge(){
        return this.userAge;
    }
    public void setUserAge(int userAge){
        this.userAge=userAge;
    }
}
```

As the userAge is a Java integer, JSF will automatically convert the inserted age to this type (notice that we did not indicate any conversion in the previous code). This is called an implicit conversion. In the case that the inserted age is not an integer, this will be reflected by an error message exposed by the h:message component.

Now, speaking of explicit conversion we can enforce the previous situation by using the UIComponent converter attribute or f:converter tag nested within a UIComponent. The modifications are reflected in the next two lines:

```
<!-- explicit conversion using the UIComponent converter attribute -->
<h:inputText id="userAgeID" required="true"
             value="#{userBean.userAge}"
             converter="javax.faces.Integer">
</h:inputText>
<!-- converter tag nested within a UIComponent -->
<h:inputText id="userAgeID" required="true"
             value="#{userBean.userAge}">
  <f:converter converterId="javax.faces.Integer"/>
</h:inputText>
```

How it works...

There is no trick here! In the case of implicit conversion, JSF tries to identify which is the appropriate converter to be applied. Obviously, for explicit conversion, JSF tries to apply the indicated converter. When conversion fails, the form is redisplayed and an exception message is fired. Otherwise, the application follows its normal flow.

There's more...

You can mix explicit and implicit conversion over the same managed bean property, but, in this case, you should keep in mind the Java cast rules. For example, if you try to explicitly force an `integer` to a `Byte` type you will get an error, as `java.lang.Integer` type can't be cast to `java.lang.Byte` type, while a `java.lang.Integer` can be cast to `java.lang.Double`.

See also

The code bundled with this book contains a complete example of this recipe. The project can be opened with NetBeans 6.8 and is named: `Working_with_implicit_and_explicit_conversion`.

Standard converters for numbers

Numbers are a generic notion used to quantify many things, such as age, salary, percent, currency, custom pattern, and so on. Also, we know that numbers can be integers, floats, doubles, and so on. Depending on what we represent, we know what kind of number to use and how to write it in the correct format and with the correct symbols attached. In this recipe you will see how to accomplish this task using JSF standard capabilities. For this we will take a generic `double` number and we will output it to represent different things.

Getting ready

We developed this recipe with NetBeans 6.8, JSF 2.0, and GlassFish v3. The JSF 2.0 classes were obtained from the NetBeans JSF 2.0 bundled library.

How to do it...

Converting numbers and applying basic formats to them are tasks that can be accomplished by the `f:convertNumber` JSF converter. This converter can be customized using a set of attributes, listed next:

Attribute name	Description
`type`	Represents the type of number. By default this type is set to `number`, but you can set it to `currency` or `percent`.
`pattern`	Represents the decimal format pattern used to convert this number.
`locale`	Represents the locale to be used for displaying this number. The user's current locale is overridden.
`maxIntegerDigits`	Represents the maximum number of integer digits to display.
`minIntegerDigits`	Represents the minimum number of integer digits to display.

Attribute name	Description
maxFractionDigits	Represents the maximum number of fractional digits to display.
minFractionDigits	Represents the minimum number of fractional digits to display.
currencyCode	Represents a three-digit international currency code when the attribute `type` is `currency`.
currenySymbol	Represents a symbol, like $, to be used when the attribute `type` is `currency`.
integerOnly	Set the value of this attribute to `true`, if you want to ignore the fractional part of a number. By default it is set to `false`.
groupingUsed	Set the value of this attribute to `true`, if you want to use a grouping symbol like comma or space. By default it is set to `true`.

Now, let's suppose that we have the number 12345.12345 (five integer digits and five fraction digits). The following code will output this number using the `f:convertNumber` converter and the previously listed attributes:

```xml
<?xml version='1.0' encoding='UTF-8' ?>
<!DOCTYPE html PUBLIC "-//W3C//DTD XHTML 1.0 Transitional//EN"
"http://www.w3.org/TR/xhtml1/DTD/xhtml1-transitional.dtd">
<html xmlns="http://www.w3.org/1999/xhtml"
      xmlns:ui="http://java.sun.com/jsf/facelets"
      xmlns:h="http://java.sun.com/jsf/html"
      xmlns:f="http://java.sun.com/jsf/core">
<h:head>
  <title>Standard converters for numbers - format numbers</title>
</h:head>
<h:body>
  <b><h:outputText value="-Formatting the double
                                  value 12345.12345-"/></b><br />
      <!-- Format as 00000.00000 -->
      <h:outputText value="Format as 00000.00000: "/>
      <h:outputText value="#{numbersBean.doubleNumber}">
          <f:convertNumber type="number" maxIntegerDigits="5"
                           maxFractionDigits="5"
                           groupingUsed="false"/>
      </h:outputText>
      <br />
      <!-- Format as 00000 -->
      <h:outputText value="Format as 00000: "/>
      <h:outputText value="#{numbersBean.doubleNumber}">
          <f:convertNumber type="number" maxIntegerDigits="5"
                           maxFractionDigits="0"/>
      </h:outputText>
      <br />
```

```
        <!-- Format as currency -->
        <h:outputText value="Format as currency: "/>
        <h:outputText value="#{numbersBean.doubleNumber}">
            <f:convertNumber type="currency" currencySymbol="$"
                             maxIntegerDigits="5"
                             maxFractionDigits="2"/>
        </h:outputText>
        <br />
        <!-- Format as percent -->
        <h:outputText value="Format as percent: "/>
        <h:outputText value="#{numbersBean.doubleNumber}">
            <f:convertNumber type="percent" maxIntegerDigits="5"
                             maxFractionDigits="5"/>
        </h:outputText>
        <br />
        <!-- Format as pattern #####,00% -->
        <h:outputText value="Format as pattern #####,00%: "/>
        <h:outputText value="#{numbersBean.doubleNumber}">
            <f:convertNumber pattern="#####,00%"/>
        </h:outputText>
    </h:body>
</html>
```

The `NumbersBean` is the managed bean, as shown next:

```
package numbers;
import javax.faces.bean.ManagedBean;
import javax.faces.bean.SessionScoped;
@ManagedBean
@SessionScoped
public class NumbersBean {
    private double doubleNumber = 12345.12345;
    public double getDoubleNumber(){
        return this.doubleNumber;
    }
    public void setDoubleNumber(double doubleNumber){
        this.doubleNumber=doubleNumber;
    }
}
```

The output will be as follows:

```
-Formatting the double value 12345.12345-
 Format as 00000.00000: 12345.12345
 Format as 00000: 12,345
 Format as currency: $12,345.12
 Format as percent: 34,512.345%
 Format as pattern #####,00%: 1,23,45,12%
```

How it works...

The number is displayed corresponding to the formatting attributes. The parts of the number that don't correspond to the conversion's restrictions are ignored or an error message is generated.

There's more...

Notice that we have used the `f:convertNumber` with the `h:outputText` component, but you can follow the same logic to use with the `h:inputText` component. These two components are the most used in conjunction with the `f:convertNumber` converter.

See also

The code bundled with this book contains a complete example of this recipe. The project can be opened with NetBeans 6.8 and is named: `Standard_converters_for_numbers`.

Standard converters for date and time

Measuring, representing, formatting, and localizing date and time was always an important issue for developers. In this recipe, you will see how to get different formats for date and time using JSF standard converters. We will display a date/time in different formats and for different locales.

Getting ready

We developed this recipe with NetBeans 6.8, JSF 2.0, and GlassFish v3. The JSF 2.0 classes were obtained from the NetBeans JSF 2.0 bundled library.

How to do it...

JSF provides a dedicated converter to accomplish tasks related to date and time, named `converterDateTime`. This converter can be customized through a set of attributes listed in the following table:

Attribute name	Description
type	Specifies whether to display the date, time, or both.
dateStyle	Specifies the formatting style for the date portion of the string. Supported values are medium (this is the default), short, long, and full. Only valid if attribute type is set.
timeStyle	Specifies the formatting style for the time portion of the string. Valid options are medium (this is the default), short, long, and full. Only valid if attribute type is set.
timeZone	Specifies the time zone for the date (For example, EST). By default GMT will be used.
locale	Specifies the locale to use for displaying the date (For example, Romania - "ro", Germany - "de", England - "en". Overrides the user's current locale.
pattern	Represents a date format pattern used to convert a number.

Now, let's suppose that we have the current date (provided by a `java.util.Date` instance). The next code will output this date using the `f:converterDateTime` converter and the previously listed attributes:

```xml
<?xml version='1.0' encoding='UTF-8' ?>
<!DOCTYPE html PUBLIC "-//W3C//DTD XHTML 1.0 Transitional//EN"
"http://www.w3.org/TR/xhtml1/DTD/xhtml1-transitional.dtd">
<html xmlns="http://www.w3.org/1999/xhtml"
      xmlns:ui="http://java.sun.com/jsf/facelets"
      xmlns:h="http://java.sun.com/jsf/html"
      xmlns:f="http://java.sun.com/jsf/core">
    <h:head>
        <title>Standard converters for date and time</title>
    </h:head>
    <h:body>
      <b><h:outputText value="-Formatting the current date
                                          and time-"/></b><br />
      <h:outputText value="#{datetimeBean.currentdate}">
        <f:convertDateTime type="date" dateStyle="medium"/>
      </h:outputText>
      <br />
      <h:outputText value="#{datetimeBean.currentdate}">
        <f:convertDateTime type="date" dateStyle="full"/>
```

```
      </h:outputText>
      <br />
      <h:outputText value="#{datetimeBean.currentdate}">
        <f:convertDateTime type="time" timeStyle="full"/>
      </h:outputText>
      <br />
      <h:outputText value="#{datetimeBean.currentdate}">
        <f:convertDateTime type="date" pattern="dd/mm/yyyy"/>
      </h:outputText>
      <br />
      <h:outputText value="#{datetimeBean.currentdate}">
        <f:convertDateTime dateStyle="full" pattern="yyyy-mm-dd"/>
      </h:outputText>
      <br />
      <h:outputText value="#{datetimeBean.currentdate}">
        <f:convertDateTime dateStyle="full"
                           pattern="yyyy.MM.dd 'at' HH:mm:ss z"/>
      </h:outputText>
      <br />
      <h:outputText value="#{datetimeBean.currentdate}">
        <f:convertDateTime dateStyle="full" pattern="h:mm a"/>
      </h:outputText>
      <br />
      <h:outputText value="#{datetimeBean.currentdate}">
        <f:convertDateTime dateStyle="long"
                           timeZone="EST" type="both" />
      </h:outputText>
      <br />
      <h:outputText value="#{datetimeBean.currentdate}">
        <f:convertDateTime locale="ro"
                           timeStyle="long" type="both"
                           dateStyle="full" />
      </h:outputText>
      <br />
      <h:outputText value="#{datetimeBean.currentdate}">
        <f:convertDateTime locale="de"
                           timeStyle="short" type="both"
                           dateStyle="full" />
      </h:outputText>
    </h:body>
</html>
```

The `datetimeBean` is listed next:

```
package datetime;
import javax.faces.bean.ManagedBean;
import javax.faces.bean.SessionScoped;
import java.util.Date;
@ManagedBean
@SessionScoped
public class DatetimeBean {
    private Date currentdate = new Date();
    public Date getCurrentdate(){
        return this.currentdate;
    }
    public void setCurrentdate(Date currentdate){
        this.currentdate=currentdate;
    }
}
```

The output will be as follows:

```
-Formatting the current date and time-
Jun 15, 2009
Monday, June 15, 2009
11:14:53 AM GMT
15/14/2009
2009-14-15
2009.06.15 at 11:14:53 GMT
11:14 AM
June 15, 2009 6:14:53 AM
15 iunie 2009 11:14:53 GMT
Montag, 15. Juni 2009 11:14
```

See also

The code bundled with this book contains a complete example of this recipe. The project can be opened with NetBeans 6.8 and is named: `Standard_converters_for_date_and_time`.

Converters and NULL values

The idea of this recipe originates in the following JSF concept: a converter with NULL values is bypassed.

The problem occurs when we want to render a special message for a NULL property, instead of returning an empty `String` or a NULL value. At first view, a custom converter should fix the problem in an elegant manner, but at second view we notice that the NULL values never get called in the converter, which means that we can't control it before the render phase. This recipe proposes a solution to this problem.

Getting ready

We have developed this recipe with NetBeans 6.8, JSF 2.0, and GlassFish v3. The JSF 2.0 classes were obtained from the NetBeans JSF 2.0 bundled library.

How to do it...

The idea is to have a placebo object—an object that it is not NULL and which is passed to the converter instead of every NULL object. The converter can identify this object by a fixed property, for example its hash code, and every time it gets this object, it will return a custom message to be rendered. For example, if our objects are instances of `java.util.Date`, then we can write a placebo class like the following one:

```
//placebo class for java.util.Date
class Placebo extends java.util.Date {
    @Override
    public int hashCode() {
        return 0011001100;
    }
    @Override
    public boolean equals(Object obj) {
        if (obj == null) {
            return false;
        }
        if (getClass() != obj.getClass()) {
            return false;
        }
        final Placebo other = (Placebo) obj;
        return true;
    }
}
```

Notice that we have arbitrarily chosen a fixed hash code as 0011001100. This hash code will mark the NULL values in the converter's `getAsString` method. However before that, we need to modify the getter method for our property as shown next (this is the entire bean, but we are focused on the `getCurrentdate` method):

```
package nullconv;
import javax.faces.bean.ManagedBean;
import javax.faces.bean.SessionScoped;
import java.util.Date;
@ManagedBean
@SessionScoped
public class NullBean {
    //valid date
    //private Date currentdate = new Date();
    //null date
    private Date currentdate = null;
    //placebo date
    private Date nulldate = new Placebo();
    public Date getCurrentdate() {
        if (currentdate == null) {
            return nulldate;
        }
        return this.currentdate;
    }
    public void setCurrentdate(Date currentdate) {
        this.currentdate = currentdate;
    }
}
```

Now, the converter gets a real date, when the `currentdate` property is not NULL, and it gets the placebo `nulldate`, when the `currentdate` property is NULL. Now, we know that the converter gets all the values, including the NULL ones. Next, the converter (`getAsString` method) will check the hash code of the objects, to see which one is NULL and which one is not. The following is the source code for this converter:

```
package nullconv;
import javax.faces.component.UIComponent;
import javax.faces.context.FacesContext;
import javax.faces.convert.ConverterException;
import javax.faces.convert.DateTimeConverter;
import javax.faces.convert.FacesConverter;
@FacesConverter(value = "nullConverter")
public class NullConverter extends DateTimeConverter {
    @Override
    public String getAsString(FacesContext arg0,
```

```
                    UIComponent arg1, Object arg2) {
        if (arg0 == null)
          {throw new NullPointerException("context");}
        if (arg1 == null)
          {throw new NullPointerException("component");}
        if (arg2 != null && !(arg2 instanceof java.util.Date)) {
            throw new ConverterException("Not valid date");
        }
        if (arg2.hashCode() == 0011001100) {
            return ("Not available!");
        }
        return super.getAsString(arg0, arg1, arg2);
    }
    @Override
    public Object getAsObject(FacesContext arg0,
                    UIComponent arg1, String arg2) {
        if (arg0 == null)
          {throw new NullPointerException("context");}
        if (arg1 == null)
          {throw new NullPointerException("component");}
        return super.getAsObject(arg0, arg1, arg2);
    }
}
```

Now, the NULL values will be rendered with a `"Not available!"` message!

How it works...

Every time a NULL date is loaded into the bean it is replaced by the placebo date. This date has the particularity of having a well known hash code. When the placebo object gets into the converter, the `getAsString` method checks for this hash code. When it finds a match it returns a custom message instead of the `String` representation of the date, because it knows that the received value is actually a NULL one, which should not be rendered verbatim.

See also

The code bundled with this book contains a complete example of this recipe. The project can be opened with NetBeans 6.8 and is named: `Converters_and_NULL_values`.

Creating and using a custom converter

JSF custom converters run on the server/client side and can accomplish many specific business needs. Basically, JSF custom converters are created by extending the `javax.faces.convert.Converter` interface or by extending a standard converter class. In this recipe, you will see both cases.

Getting ready

We developed this recipe with NetBeans 6.8, JSF 2.0, and GlassFish v3. The JSF 2.0 classes were obtained from the NetBeans JSF 2.0 bundled library.

How to do it...

First, let's talk about the converters that implement the `Converters` interface. In this case, a converter should implement two methods, as follows:

The `getAsObject` method takes the `FacesContext` instance, the UI component, and the `String` to be converted to a specified object. According to the official documentation, this method:

> *Converts the specified string value, which is associated with the specified* `UIComponent`, *into a model data object that is appropriate for being stored during the* `Apply Request Values` *phase of the request processing lifecycle.*

```
public Object getAsObject(FacesContext context,
                          UIComponent component,
                          java.lang.String value){

    ...
}
```

The `getAsString` method takes the `FacesContext` instance, the UI component, and the object to be converted to a `String`. According to the official documentation, this method:

> *Converts the specified model object value, which is associated with the specified* `UIComponent`, *into a String that is suitable for being included in the response generated during the* `Render Response` *phase of the request processing lifecycle.*

```
public String getAsString(FacesContext context,
                          UIComponent component,
                          Object value){

    ...
}
```

This converter logic should use `javax.faces.converter.ConverterException` to throw the appropriate exceptions and `javax.faces.application.FacesMessage` to generate the corresponding error messages.

For example, the following custom converter will convert a `java.util.Date` into a format of type `yyyy-MM-dd`. This implementation will extend the `Converter` interface, as shown next:

```java
package datetime;
import java.text.DateFormat;
import java.text.ParseException;
import java.text.SimpleDateFormat;
import java.util.Calendar;
import java.util.Date;
import javax.faces.application.FacesMessage;
import javax.faces.component.UIComponent;
import javax.faces.context.FacesContext;
import javax.faces.convert.Converter;
import javax.faces.convert.ConverterException;
import javax.faces.convert.FacesConverter;
@FacesConverter(value = "customDateConverterImpl")
public class CustomDateConverterImpl implements Converter {
    public String getAsString(FacesContext arg0, UIComponent arg1,
Object arg2) {
        if (arg0 == null) {
            throw new NullPointerException("context");
        }
        if (arg1 == null) {
            throw new NullPointerException("component");
        }
        final Date date = (Date) arg2;
        String DATE_FORMAT = "yyyy-MM-dd";
        SimpleDateFormat sdf =
                new SimpleDateFormat(DATE_FORMAT);
        Calendar c1 = Calendar.getInstance(); // today
        c1.setTime(date);
        return sdf.format(c1.getTime());
    }
    public Object getAsObject(FacesContext arg0, UIComponent arg1,
String arg2) {
        if (arg0 == null) {
            throw new NullPointerException("context");
        }
        if (arg1 == null) {
            throw new NullPointerException("component");
        }
```

```
        DateFormat df = new SimpleDateFormat("yyyy-MM-dd");
        try {
            Date today = df.parse(arg2);
            return today;
        } catch (ParseException e) {
            FacesMessage message = new FacesMessage(FacesMessage.
SEVERITY_ERROR,
                    "Parser error!", "Cannot parse this date!");
            throw new ConverterException(message);
        }
    }
}
```

The previous converter can be called from an XHTML page as shown next (notice that we pass to the `converter` attribute the `value` from the `@FacesConverter` annotation; this annotation defines a name for a converter and it is specific to JSF 2.0):

```
<h:form id="customDateTimeID">
  <h:inputText id="dateID" value="#{datetimeBean.currentdate}"
            converter="customDateConverterImpl">
  </h:inputText>
  <h:message showSummary="true" showDetail="false" for="dateID"
            style="color: red; text-decoration:overline"/>
  <br />
  <h:commandButton value="Submit"
                action="selected?faces-redirect=true"/>
</h:form>
```

Now, let's discuss converters that extend existing converters. In this case, we override the `getAsString` and `getAsObject` methods (mark them with the `@Override` annotation) or we can call setter methods from the extended converter. For example, we can extend the `DateTimeConverter` and call the `setPattern` to obtain the same effect as the previous converter.

```
package datetime;
import java.util.TimeZone;
import javax.faces.convert.DateTimeConverter;
import javax.faces.convert.FacesConverter;
@FacesConverter(value = "customDateConverterExtend")
public class CustomDateConverterExtend extends DateTimeConverter {
  public CustomDateConverterExtend() {
    super();
    setTimeZone(TimeZone.getDefault());
    setPattern("yyyy-MM-dd");
  }
}
```

How it works...

A JSF converter is called from two directions. It is called once during the `Apply Request Values Phase` and once during the `Render Response Phase`. In `Apply Request Values Phase` the converter is called through `getAsObject` method, which is responsible to for converting the user inputs, while in the `Render Response` the converter is called through the `getAsString` method, which is responsible to for converting outputs before rendering.

There's more...

Keep in mind that in JSF 2.0 we don't need a `faces-config.xml` descriptor, and converters need not be declared in any XML file. If you are using JSF 1.2 then you have to register converters in the `faces-config.xml` document following the syntax listed next:

```
<converter>
  <converter-id>CONVERTER_ID</converter-id>
  <converter-class>CONVERTER_CLASS_NAME</converter-class>
</converter>
```

See also

The code bundled with this book contains a complete example of this recipe. The project can be opened with NetBeans 6.8 and it is named: `Creating_and_using_a_custom_converter`.

Using custom converters for h:selectOneMenu

A common issue regarding JSF converters and the `h:selectOneMenu` component can be recreated in a simple scenario. Let's suppose that we are in the following situation: we have a database table that contains a number of rows that define cars. Each row has an `Integer` value representing the car number and a `string` value representing the car name. Obviously this table is wrapped into a managed bean, as shown next:

```
package cars;
import javax.faces.bean.ManagedBean;
@ManagedBean
public class CarBean {
  private Integer carNumber;
  private String carName;
  public CarBean() {}
  public CarBean(Integer carNumber, String carName){
    this.carNumber=carNumber;
```

```
      this.carName=carName;
    }
    public Integer getCarNumber(){
      return this.carNumber;
    }
    public void setCarNumber(Integer carNumber){
      this.carNumber=carNumber;
    }
    public String getCarName(){
      return this.carName;
    }
    public void setCarName(String carName){
      this.carName=carName;
    }
  }
}
```

Going further, let's have another managed bean that contains a collection of cars (we simulate the table database with a few manual instances), as shown next:

```
package cars;
import java.util.HashMap;
import java.util.LinkedList;
import java.util.List;
import javax.faces.bean.ManagedBean;
import javax.faces.bean.SessionScoped;
import javax.faces.model.SelectItem;
@ManagedBean(name = "carsBean")
@SessionScoped
public class CarsBean {
  private HashMap<Integer, CarBean> myCars =
                                    new HashMap<Integer, CarBean>();
    private List<SelectItem> carItems = new LinkedList<SelectItem>();
    private CarBean selectedCar;
    public CarsBean() {
        CarBean car_1 = new CarBean(1, "Ferrari");
        CarBean car_2 = new CarBean(2, "Logan");
        CarBean car_3 = new CarBean(3, "Fiat");
        CarBean car_4 = new CarBean(4, "Kia");
        CarBean car_5 = new CarBean(5, "Skoda");
        carItems.add(new SelectItem(car_1, car_1.getCarName()));
        myCars.put(car_1.getCarNumber(), car_1);
        carItems.add(new SelectItem(car_2, car_2.getCarName()));
        myCars.put(car_2.getCarNumber(), car_2);
        carItems.add(new SelectItem(car_3, car_3.getCarName()));
        myCars.put(car_3.getCarNumber(), car_3);
```

```
        carItems.add(new SelectItem(car_4, car_4.getCarName()));
        myCars.put(car_4.getCarNumber(), car_4);
        carItems.add(new SelectItem(car_5, car_5.getCarName()));
        myCars.put(car_5.getCarNumber(), car_5);
    }
    public CarBean getCar(Integer number) {
        return (CarBean) myCars.get(number);
    }
    public List<SelectItem> getCarItems() {
        return carItems;
    }
    public void setCarItems(List<SelectItem> carItems) {
        this.carItems = carItems;
    }
    public CarBean getSelectedCar() {
        return this.selectedCar;
    }
    public void setSelectedCar(CarBean selectedCar) {
        this.selectedCar = selectedCar;
    }
}
```

Now, we can render our car collection using an `h:selectOneMenu` component, as shown next:

```
<h:form id="selectCarFormID">
 <h:selectOneMenu id="carsID" value="#{carsBean.selectedCar}">
  <f:selectItems value="#{carsBean.carItems}"/>
 </h:selectOneMenu>
 <h:commandButton value="Submit" action="selected?faces-
     redirect=true"/>
</h:form>
```

Well, the car list is rendered OK, as you can see the list and make a selection. However, the problem occurs when we choose a car and we try to populate the `selectedCar` property with it. As you see, the `selectedCar` is a `CarBean` instance, while the submitted information represents an integer (the car number). Therefore, we need to convert this integer to a `CarBean`, before it gets rendered, as shown next:

```
<h:outputText value="Selected car number:"/>
<h:outputText value="#{carsBean.selectedCar.carNumber}"/>
   <br />
<h:outputText value="Selected car name:"/>
<h:outputText value="#{carsBean.selectedCar.carName}"/>
```

Getting ready

We developed this recipe with NetBeans 6.8, JSF 2.0, and GlassFish v3. The JSF 2.0 classes were obtained from the NetBeans JSF 2.0 bundled library.

How to do it...

The solution came from a custom converter. In the getAsString object, we extract and return the car number, and in the getAsObject method, the submitted car number is converted into a CarBean instance, as shown in the following code:

```
package cars;
import javax.el.ValueExpression;
import javax.faces.application.FacesMessage;
import javax.faces.component.UIComponent;
import javax.faces.context.FacesContext;
import javax.faces.convert.Converter;
import javax.faces.convert.ConverterException;
import javax.faces.convert.FacesConverter;
@FacesConverter(value = "carConverter")
public class CarConverter implements Converter {
    public String getAsString(
                   FacesContext arg0, UIComponent arg1, Object arg2) {
        if (arg0 == null){throw new NullPointerException("context");}
        if (arg1 == null){throw new NullPointerException("component");}
        return ((CarBean)arg2).getCarNumber().toString();
    }
    public Object getAsObject(
                   FacesContext arg0, UIComponent arg1, String arg2) {
        if (arg0 == null){throw new NullPointerException("context");}
        if (arg1 == null){throw new NullPointerException("component");}
        FacesContext ctx = FacesContext.getCurrentInstance();
        ValueExpression vex =
        ctx.getApplication().getExpressionFactory()
                       .createValueExpression(ctx.getELContext(),
                                        "#{carsBean}",CarsBean.class);
        CarsBean cars = (CarsBean)vex.getValue(ctx.getELContext());
        CarBean car;
        try {
        car = cars.getCar(new Integer (arg2));
        } catch( NumberFormatException e ) {
        FacesMessage message =
          new FacesMessage(FacesMessage.SEVERITY_ERROR,
          "Unknown value", "This is not a car number!" );
           throw new ConverterException( message );
        }
        if( car == null ) {
```

```
FacesMessage message = new FacesMessage(
                                 FacesMessage.SEVERITY_ERROR,
    "Unknown value", "The car is unknown!" );
    throw new ConverterException( message );
  }
  return car;
  }
}
```

How it works...

The mechanism is pretty simple! First, the collection of cars is rendered using a `SelectItem` object. Every single car will pass through the converter's `getAsString` method and is added to the list. Notice that the `getAsString` method extracts and returns the car number for each car.

Second, when a car is selected and submitted, the selected car number arrives into the `getAsObject` method. There we search for the corresponding car into our `myCars` map. Once the car is found it is returned into the `setSelectedCar` method.

There's more...

You can use the same technique for `h:selectManyCheckbox` or `h:selectManyListbox`. For example, in the case of `h:selectManyCheckbox`, you will render the list in the following way:

```
<h:form id="selectCarFormID">
 <h:selectManyCheckbox id="carsID"
                       value="#{carsBean.selectedCar}"
                       converter="carConverter">
   <f:selectItems value="#{carsBean.carItems}"/>
 </h:selectManyCheckbox>
 <h:commandButton value="Submit"
                  action="selected?faces-redirect=true"/>
</h:form>
```

And the selections can be rendered, as shown next:

```
<h:dataTable  value="#{carsBean.selectedCar}" var="item">
  <h:column>
    <f:facet name="header">
      <h:outputText value="Car Name:"/>
    </f:facet>
    <h:outputText value="#{item.carName}"/>
  </h:column>
</h:dataTable>
```

See also

The code bundled with this book contains a complete example of this recipe. The project can be opened with NetBeans 6.8 and is named: `Using_custom_converters_for_selectOneMenu_1` and `Using_custom_converters_for_selectOneMenu_2`.

Binding converters to backing bean properties

JSF standard converter tags allow binding attributes (this is also true for listener and validator tags). This means that developers can bind converter implementations to backing bean properties. The main advantages of using the binding facility are:

▶ The developer can allow the backing bean to instantiate the implementation

▶ The backing bean can programmatically access the implementation's attributes

Getting ready

We developed this recipe with NetBeans 6.8, JSF 2.0, and GlassFish v3. The JSF 2.0 classes were obtained from the NetBeans JSF 2.0 bundled library.

How to do it...

To successfully accomplish a binding task, you can follow the three simple steps listed next (these steps are true for converter, listener, and validator tags):

1. Nest the converter (listener, validator) tag in the component tag.
2. Put in the backing bean a property that takes and returns the converter (listener, validator) implementation class.
3. Reference the backing bean property using a value expression from the `binding` attribute of the converter (listener, validator) tag.

For example, let's bind the standard `convertNumber` converter to a backing bean property. The idea is to let the backing bean set the formatting pattern of the user's input. First, you have to register the converter onto the component by nesting the `convertNumber` tag within the component tag. Then, you have to reference the property with the `binding` attribute of the `convertNumber` tag, as shown next:

```
<h:form id="numberFormID">
  <h:inputText id="numberID" value="#{numbersBean.numbery}">
    <f:convertNumber binding="#{numbersBean.number}" />
  </h:inputText>
```

```
    <h:message showSummary="true" showDetail="false" for="numberID"
            style="color: red; text-decoration:overline"/>
    <br />
    <h:commandButton value="Submit"
                    action="selected?faces-redirect=true"/>
</h:form>
```

The `number` property would be similar to the following code:

```
package numbers;
import javax.faces.bean.ManagedBean;
import javax.faces.bean.SessionScoped;
import javax.faces.convert.NumberConverter;
@ManagedBean
@SessionScoped
public class NumbersBean {
    private NumberConverter number;
    private float numbery;
public float getNumbery(){
    return this.numbery;
 }
public void setNumbery(float numbery){
    this.numbery=numbery;
 }
public NumberConverter getNumber(){
    return this.number;
 }
public void setNumber(NumberConverter number){
    number.setType("currency");
    number.setCurrencySymbol("$");
    this.number=number;
 }
}
```

How it works...

In our example, the backing bean sets the formatting pattern within the `convertNumber` tag, which means that the user's input will be constrained to this pattern. This time the numbers are formatted as currencies, without using specific attributes in the `convertNumber` tag. Instead of this we use the `binding` attribute to reference the number property, which is a `NumberConverter` instance, offering us access to this class's methods.

See also

The code bundled with this book contains a complete example of this recipe. The project can be opened with NetBeans 6.8 and is named: `Bind_converters_to_backing_bean_ properties`.

RichFaces and standard converters

This recipe will show you how to use one of the standard converters defined in RichFaces. First you have to know that RichFaces 3.3.3 comes with a set of converters that can be found in the following packages:

- `org.richfaces.convert`
- `org.richfaces.convert.rowkey`
- `org.richfaces.convert.seamtext`
- `org.richfaces.convert.seamtext.tags`
- `org.richfaces.convert.selection`
- `org.richfaces.converter`

In this recipe, we will use the `org.richfaces.convert.IntegerColorConverter` for converting an RGB color from a RichFaces `ColorPicker` component into an integer and vice versa.

Getting ready

We developed this recipe with NetBeans 6.8, JSF 2.0, and GlassFish v3. The JSF 2.0 classes were obtained from the NetBeans JSF 2.0 bundled library. In addition, we have used RichFaces 3.3.3.BETA1, which provides support for JSF 2.0. You can download this distribution from `http://www.jboss.org/richfaces`. The RichFaces libraries (including necessary dependencies) are in the book code bundle, under the `|JSF_libs|RichFaces - JSF 2.0` folder.

How to do it...

In RichFaces, we can use the `converter` attribute or `f:converter` tag nested within a `UIComponent`. This is pretty similar to the JSF standard utilization of converters. For example, in the following code we have a `colorPicker` component and we apply the `IntegerColorConverter` converter to the selected color using the `converter` attribute. The result of conversion is an integer representation of the color and it is rendered into an `outputText` component:

```
<a4j:form>
 <h:outputText value="The integer version of
   the selected color:"/>
 <h:outputText id="RGBvalue" value="#{colorPickerBean.color}"/>
 <rich:panel header="RichFaces Color Picker"
   style="width: 315px">
  <rich:colorPicker value="#{colorPickerBean.color}"
    colorMode="rgb" converter="org.richfaces.IntegerColor">
    <a4j:support event="onchange" reRender="RGBvalue"/>
  </rich:colorPicker>
 </rich:panel>
</a4j:form>
```

Notice that the `IntegerColorConverter` ID is `org.richfaces.IntegerColor`. You can find the converters' IDs in the Javadoc of RichFaces.

The `ColorPickerBean` can be written in the following way:

```
package colorpicker;
public class ColorPickerBean {
  private Integer color;
  /**
   * @return ColorPickerBean color
   */
  public Integer getColor() {
    return color;
  }
  /**
   * @param ColorPickerBean color
   */
  public void setColor(Integer color) {
    this.color = color;
  }
}
```

How it works...

It works exactly like a JSF standard converter. If the value passes the conversion phase, then the backing bean receives the converted value, otherwise the user gets an error message and the option to try again.

See also

The code bundled with this book contains a complete example of this recipe. The project can be opened with NetBeans 6.8 and it is named: `RichFaces_standard_and_custom_converters`.

RichFaces and custom converters

In this recipe, we will develop and use a custom converter in RichFaces. This will convert an RGB color, extracted from a `colorPicker`, into an integer similar to the result of the `java.awt.Color.getRGB` method and vice versa. The result is rendered with an `outputText` component.

Notice that an RGB color from a `colorPicker` is a `String` formatted as `rgb(red, green, blue)`.

Getting ready

We developed this recipe with NetBeans 6.8, JSF 2.0, and GlassFish v3. The JSF 2.0 classes were obtained from the NetBeans JSF 2.0 bundled library. In addition, we have used RichFaces 3.3.3.BETA1, which provides support for JSF 2.0. You can download this distribution from `http://www.jboss.org/richfaces`. The RichFaces libraries (including necessary dependencies) are in the book code bundle, under the `|JSF_libs|RichFaces - JSF 2.0` folder.

How to do it...

A RichFaces custom converter follows the same principles as a JSF custom converter. We can implement the `Converter` interface or extend an existing converter class. For example, in this case we will implement the `Converter` interface and we will implement the `getAsString` and `getAsObject` methods. As the code is self-explanatory there is no need for more details:

```
package colorpicker;
import java.awt.Color;
import javax.faces.component.UIComponent;
import javax.faces.context.FacesContext;
import javax.faces.convert.Converter;
import java.util.StringTokenizer;
public class RGBConverter implements Converter {
public static final String CONVERTER_ID = "rgbConverter";
public Object getAsObject(FacesContext context, UIComponent component,
String value) {
```

```
if (context == null) {
    throw new NullPointerException("context");
    }
if (component == null) {
    throw new NullPointerException("component");
    }
String getRGBfromString = value.substring(4, value.length() - 1);
StringTokenizer rgbComponents = new StringTokenizer(getRGBfromString,
",");
int r = Integer.valueOf(rgbComponents.nextToken().trim());
int g = Integer.valueOf(rgbComponents.nextToken().trim());
int b = Integer.valueOf(rgbComponents.nextToken().trim());
Color rgbColor = new Color(r, g, b);
int rgbValue = rgbColor.getRGB();
Integer rgbValueInt = new Integer(rgbValue);
return rgbValueInt;
}
public String getAsString(FacesContext context, UIComponent component,
Object value) {
if (context == null) {
    throw new NullPointerException("context");
    }
if (component == null) {
    throw new NullPointerException("component");
    }
Color rgbColor = new Color((Integer) value);
String stringRGB = "rgb(" + rgbColor.getRed() + ","
+ rgbColor.getGreen() + "," + rgbColor.getBlue() + ")";
return stringRGB;
    }
}
```

Calling this converter is a simple task that we have accomplished as shown next:

```
<a4j:form>
 <h:outputText value="The integer version of the
  selected color:"/>
<h:outputText id="RGBvalue" value="#{colorPickerBean.color}"/>
<rich:panel header="RichFaces Color Picker" style="width: 315px">
 <rich:colorPicker value="#{colorPickerBean.color}"
   colorMode="rgb" converter="rgbConverter">
  <a4j:support event="onchange" reRender="RGBvalue"/>
 </rich:colorPicker>
</rich:panel>
</a4j:form>
```

The `ColorPickerBean` can be written in the following way:

```
package colorpicker;
public class ColorPickerBean {
private Integer color;
/**
 * @return ColorPickerBean color
 */
public Integer getColor() {
    return color;
    }
/**
 * @param ColorPickerBean color
 */
public void setColor(Integer color) {
    this.color = color;
    }
}
```

How it works...

It works exactly like a JSF custom converter. See the *How it works...* section, in the *Creating and using a custom converter* recipe.

See also

The code bundled with this book contains a complete example of this recipe. The project can be opened with NetBeans 6.8 and is named: `RichFaces_standard_and_custom_converters`.

Instance variables in converters

If you are making a simple attempt to declare an instance variable in a converter, you will notice that you can't store the variable state over time. This may look like a strange behavior, but the truth is that the `getAsObject` and `getAsString` are called on different instances. This is the simple explanation of why the instance variable doesn't have persistence over these methods calls.

We can fix this using `UIComponent set/getAttribute` or using a session variable instead. In this recipe, we will use a session variable to simulate an instance variable of a converter. For this, let's suppose that we have two numbers, one inserted by the user and one is selected by the user from a `selectOneMenu` component. The inserted value is multiplied with the selected value, inside of a custom converter, in the `getAsObject` method. In the backing bean we keep the multiplied result. Before the result is rendered, its value is divided by the same value in the `getAsString` method. If everything works fine, then we will not notice these operations over the inserted value.

Getting ready

We developed this recipe with NetBeans 6.8, JSF 2.0, and GlassFish v3. The JSF 2.0 classes were obtained from the NetBeans JSF 2.0 bundled library.

How to do it...

Storing the selected value in the session is a simple task. First, the backing bean associated to this value is marked with the annotation `@SessionScoped`, indicating that the instance of this bean should be stored in session. Second, we pass the selected value in the traditional way (this code is from the `multiply.xhtml` page of the application), as shown next:

```
<h:form id="MultiplyForm">
 <h:outputText value="Select the multiply factor:" />
 <h:selectOneMenu id="factorID"
                  value="#{factorBean.selectedFactor}">
  <f:selectItems value="#{factorBean.factors}"/>
 </h:selectOneMenu>
 <h:commandButton id="submit" action=
                      "number?faces-redirect=true" value="Submit"/>
</h:form>
```

The `selectedFactor` property belongs to the next backing bean:

```
package multiply;
import java.util.LinkedList;
import java.util.List;
import javax.faces.bean.ManagedBean;
import javax.faces.bean.SessionScoped;
import javax.faces.model.SelectItem;
@ManagedBean
@SessionScoped
public class FactorBean {
 private List<SelectItem> factors = new LinkedList<SelectItem>();
 private double selectedFactor;
public FactorBean(){
        factors.add(new SelectItem("1.0", "1.0"));
        factors.add(new SelectItem("2.0", "2.0"));
        factors.add(new SelectItem("3.0", "3.0"));
        factors.add(new SelectItem("4.0", "4.0"));
        factors.add(new SelectItem("5.0", "5.0"));
    }
```

```
public List<SelectItem> getFactors() {
        return factors;
    }
public void setFactors(List<SelectItem> factors) {
        this.factors = factors;
    }
public double getSelectedFactor() {
        return this.selectedFactor;
    }
public void setSelectedFactor(double selectedFactor) {
        this.selectedFactor = selectedFactor;
    }
}
```

Now, the multiplication factor is on session and we can request the user to insert a value to be multiplied by this factor (number.xhtml), as shown next:

```
<h:form id="NumberForm">
    <h:outputText value="Insert the value to be multiplied:"/>
    <h:inputText id="valueID" required="true"
                value="#{multiplyBean.value}"
                converter="multiplyConverter" />
    <h:message showSummary="true" showDetail="false" for="valueID"
                style="color: red; text-decoration:overline"/>
    <br />
    <h:commandButton id="submit" action="number?faces-
            redirect=true" value="Submit"/>
</h:form>
```

The value is stored in the MultiplyBean, as shown next:

```
package multiply;
import javax.faces.bean.ManagedBean;
import javax.faces.bean.SessionScoped;
@ManagedBean
@SessionScoped
public class MultiplyBean {
    private double value = 0.0d;
    public double getValue() {
        return this.value;
    }
    public void setValue(double value) {
        this.value = value;
    }
}
```

As you can see the operations are taking place in a converter. Now, the converter has access to the multiplication factor in a very easy approach, as shown next:

```java
public String getAsString(FacesContext arg0, UIComponent arg1,
                          Object arg2) {
    if (arg0 == null) {
            throw new NullPointerException("context");
        }
    if (arg1 == null) {
            throw new NullPointerException("component");
        }
    FacesContext ctx = FacesContext.getCurrentInstance();
    ValueExpression vex =
        ctx.getApplication().getExpressionFactory().
        createValueExpression(ctx.getELContext(),
        "#{factorBean}", FactorBean.class);
    FactorBean c = (FactorBean) vex.getValue(ctx.getELContext());
    try {
        Double dividedVal = (Double) arg2 / c.getSelectedFactor();
        return dividedVal.toString();
        } catch (Exception e) {
        FacesMessage message = new
         FacesMessage(FacesMessage.SEVERITY_ERROR,
         "Error!", "Cannot accomplish this operation (DIVIDE) !");
         throw new ConverterException(message);
        }
    }
public Object getAsObject(FacesContext arg0, UIComponent arg1, String
arg2) {
    if (arg0 == null) {
            throw new NullPointerException("context");
        }
    if (arg1 == null) {
            throw new NullPointerException("component");
        }
    FacesContext ctx = FacesContext.getCurrentInstance();
    ValueExpression vex =
        ctx.getApplication().getExpressionFactory().
        createValueExpression(ctx.getELContext(),
        "#{factorBean}", FactorBean.class);
    FactorBean c = (FactorBean) vex.getValue(ctx.getELContext());
    try {
        Double val = new Double(arg2);
        Double multiplyVal = val * c.getSelectedFactor();
        return multiplyVal;
```

```
        } catch (NumberFormatException e) {
      FacesMessage message = new
       FacesMessage(FacesMessage.SEVERITY_ERROR,
       "Error!","Connot accomplish this operation (MULTIPLY)!");
        throw new ConverterException(message);
        }
   }
```

How it works...

First, we store in the session the value that we need to have access to in the converter's methods. Second, we call this session value from the getAsString and getAsObject methods. Using this technique we have replaced the instance variable of the converter with a session variable.

See also

The code bundled with this book contains a complete example of this recipe. The project can be opened with NetBeans 6.8 and is named: Instance_variables_in_converters.

Client-side converters with MyFaces Trinidad

A great facility of Apache MyFaces Trinidad is that it supports client-side versions of JSF converters and validators. This means that errors are detected on the client machine, and the server is not involved. In this recipe, we will create such a converter for converting a number into an IP address. Our restrictions will be as follows:

- The IP address should have exactly 12 digits
- The IP will always have a pattern of 000.000.000.000
- The IP can be supplied like 000000000000 or 000.000.000.000

The idea of Apache Trinidad client conversion is that it works on the client in a very similar way to how it works on the server, but in this case the language on the client is JavaScript instead of Java. By convention, JavaScript objects are prefixed in Trindad with the tr prefix, in order to avoid name collisions. There are JavaScript converter objects that support the methods getAsString and getAsObject. A TrConverter can throw a TrConverterException.

Let's see what are the steps that should be accomplished to create such a converter.

Getting ready

We developed this recipe with NetBeans 6.8, JSF 2.0, and GlassFish v3. The JSF 2.0 classes were obtained from the NetBeans JSF 2.0 bundled library. In addition, we have used Apache Trinidad 2.0.0, which provides support for JSF 2.0. You can download this distribution from `http://myfaces.apache.org/trinidad/index.html`. The **Apache Trinidad** libraries (including necessary dependencies) are in the book code bundle, under the `|JSF_libs|Apache Trinidad - JSF 2.0` folder.

How to do it...

We will develop a complete application, including the client-side converter by following the four listed steps:

1. Develop a JavaScript version of the converter. Before doing this you have to be aware of the Trindad API, which is listed next (this can also be found on the Trinidad website `http://myfaces.apache.org/trinidad/index.html`):

```
/**
 * Converter "interface" similar to javax.faces.convert.Converter,
 * except that all relevant information must be passed to the
constructor
 * as the context and component are not passed to the getAsString
or getAsObject method
 *
 */
function TrConverter()
{
}
/**
 * Convert the specified model object value, into a String for
display
 *
 * @param value Model object value to be converted
 * @param label label to identify the editableValueHolder to the
user
 *
 * @return the value as a string or undefined in case of no
converter mechanism is
 * available (see TrNumberConverter).
 */
TrConverter.prototype.getAsString = function(value, label){}
/**
```

```
 * Convert the specified string value into a model data object
 * which can be passed to validators
 *
 * @param value String value to be converted
 * @param label label to identify the editableValueHolder to the
user
 *
 * @return the converted value or undefined in case of no
converter mechanism is
 * available (see TrNumberConverter).
 */
TrConverter.prototype.getAsObject = function(value, label){}
```

TrConverters can throw a TrConverterException, which should contain a TrFacesMessage. Here is the signature for TrFacesMessage:

```
/**
 * Message similar to javax.faces.application.FacesMessage
 *
 * @param summary - Localized summary message text
 * @param detail - Localized detail message text
 * @param severity - An optional severity for this message.  Use
constants
 *   SEVERITY_INFO, SEVERITY_WARN, SEVERITY_ERROR, and
 *   SEVERITY_FATAL from the FacesMessage class.  Default is
 *   SEVERITY_INFO
 */
function TrFacesMessage(
  summary,
  detail,
  severity
  )
```

The signature for the TrConverterException is as follows:

```
/**
 * TrConverterException is an exception thrown by the
getAsObject() or getAsString()
 * method of a Converter, to indicate that the requested
conversion cannot be performed.
 *
 * @param facesMessage the TrFacesMessage associated with this
exception
 * @param summary Localized summary message text, used to create
only if facesMessage is null
```

```
 * @param detail Localized detail message text, used only if
facesMessage is null
 */
function TrConverterException(
  facesMessage,
  summary,
  detail
  )
```

Another useful API that can be used to format messages is shown next:

```
/**
 * TrFastMessageFormatUtils is a greatly reduced version
 * of the java.text.MessageFormat class, but delivered as a
utility.
 * <p>
 * The only syntax supported by this class is simple index-based
 * replacement, namely:
 * <pre>
 *      some{1}text{0}here{2}andthere
 * </pre>
 * as well as escaping using single quotes.  Like MessageFormat,
 * a single quote must be represented using two consecutive single
 * quotes, but the contents of any text between single quotes
 * will not be interpreted.  So, the following pattern could
 * be used to include a left bracket:
 * <pre>
 *      some'{'text{0}
 * </pre>
 */
function TrFastMessageFormatUtils()
 /**
  * Formats the given array of strings based on the initial
  * pattern.
  * @param {String} String to format
  * @param {any...:undefined} Varargs objects to substitute for
positional parameters.
  * Each parameter will be converted to a String and substituted
into the format.
  */
TrFastMessageFormatUtils.format = function(
  formatString, // error format string with embedded indexes to be
replaced
```

```
    parameters    // {any...:undefined} Varargs objects to
substitute for positional parameters.
    )
```

Based on this API, we have developed the JavaScript version of our IP converter as follows (`IPConverter.js`):

```javascript
function ipGetAsString(value, label)
{
  return value.substring(0,3) + '.' + value.substring(3,6) + '.' +
value.substring(6,9) + '.' + value.substring(9,12);
}
function ipGetAsObject(value, label)
{
  if (!value)return null;
  var len=value.length;
  var messageKey = IPConverter.NOT;
  if (len < 12 )
    messageKey = IPConverter.SHORT;
  else if (len > 15)
    messageKey = IPConverter.LONG;
  else if ((len == 12)||(len == 15))
  {
      return value;
  }
  if (messageKey!=null && this._messages!=null)
  {
    // format the detail error string
    var detail = this._messages[messageKey];
    if (detail != null)
    {
      detail = TrFastMessageFormatUtils.format(detail,
                                        label, value);
    }
    var facesMessage = new TrFacesMessage(
                    this._messages[IPConverter.SUMMARY],
                    detail,
                    TrFacesMessage.SEVERITY_ERROR)
    throw new TrConverterException(facesMessage);
  }
  return null;
}
```

```
function IPConverter(messages) {
    this._messages = messages;
}
IPConverter.prototype = new TrConverter();
IPConverter.prototype.getAsString = ipGetAsString;
IPConverter.prototype.getAsObject = ipGetAsObject;
IPConverter.SUMMARY = 'SUM';
IPConverter.SHORT = 'S';
IPConverter.LONG = 'L';
IPConverter.NOT = 'N';
```

2. Next we bind the JavaScript converter with the Java converter. For this we have to implement the `org.apache.myfaces.trinidad.converter.ClientConverter` interface. The methods of this interface are:

   - `getClientLibrarySource()`: returns a library that includes an implementation of the JavaScript `Converter` object.
   - `getClientConversion()`: returns a JavaScript constructor, which will be used to instantiate an instance of the converter.
   - `getClientScript()`: can be used to write out inline JavaScript.
   - `getClientImportNames()`: is used to import the built-in scripts provided by Apache MyFaces Trinidad.

   Now, the Java version of our `IPConverter` looks like this (notice the constructor used to instantiate the JavaScript version):

```
package converterJSF;
import java.util.Collection;
import javax.faces.application.FacesMessage;
import javax.faces.component.UIComponent;
import javax.faces.context.FacesContext;
import javax.faces.convert.Converter;
import javax.faces.convert.ConverterException;
import org.apache.myfaces.trinidad.convert.ClientConverter;
import org.apache.myfaces.trinidad.util.LabeledFacesMessage;
public class IPConverter implements Converter, ClientConverter
{
  private static final String _SHORT_ERROR_TEXT = "The value is to
short for an IP of type 000.000.000.000!";
  private static final String _LONG_ERROR_TEXT = "The value is to
long for an IP of type 000.000.000.000!";
  private static final String _INVALID_ERROR_TEXT = "The value is
not a valid IP number";
```

```java
      public static final String CONVERTER_ID = "converterJSF.IP";
      //getAsObject
      public Object getAsObject(FacesContext context, UIComponent
component, String value)
   {
   if ( value == null || value.trim().length() == 0)
       return null;
       String ipValue = value.trim();
       int length = ipValue.length();
       if ( length < 12 )
       {
       throw new ConverterException(_getMessage(
                                    component, _SHORT_ERROR_TEXT));
       }
       if ( length > 15 )
       {
       throw new ConverterException(_getMessage(
                                    component, _LONG_ERROR_TEXT));
       }
      //12
       if (length == 12)
       {
        try
          {
            return Long.valueOf(ipValue);
          } catch(NumberFormatException e)
          {
            throw new ConverterException(_getMessage(
                                    component, _INVALID_ERROR_TEXT));
          }
        }
      //15
       if (length == 15)
       {
        try
          {
          String extractIP = ipValue.substring(0,3) +
          ipValue.substring(4,7) + ipValue.substring(8,11) +
          ipValue.substring(12,15);
          return Long.valueOf(extractIP);
          } catch(NumberFormatException e)
```

```
            {
                throw new ConverterException(_getMessage(
                                    component, _INVALID_ERROR_TEXT));
            }
        }
    throw new ConverterException(_getMessage(component, _INVALID_
ERROR_TEXT));
}
    //getAsString
    public String getAsString(FacesContext context, UIComponent
component, Object value)
    {
    if ( value == null || !(value instanceof Long))
        return null;
     Long longValue=(Long)value;
     String valueString = longValue.toString();
     String ip="000.000.000.000";
     if (valueString.length() == 12)
        {
        ip = valueString.substring(0,3) + '.' +
            valueString.substring(3,6) + '.' +
            valueString.substring(6,9) + '.' +
            valueString.substring(9,12);
        }
    return ip;
    }
    //implement the ClientConverter's getClientImportNames
    public Collection<String> getClientImportNames()
        {
            return null;
        }
    //implement the ClientConverter's getClientLibrarySource
    public String getClientLibrarySource(
     FacesContext context)
     {
     return context.getExternalContext().getRequestContextPath() +
            "/jsLibs/IPConverter.js";
     }
    //implement the ClientConverter's getClientConversion
    public String getClientConversion(FacesContext context,
                                    UIComponent component)
```

```
    {
    return ("new IPConverter({"
    + "SUM:'Invalid IP.',"
    + "S:'Value \"{1}\" is too short for an 000.000.000.000 IP.',"
    + "L:'Value \"{1}\" is too long for an 000.000.000.000 IP.',"
    + "N:'Value \"{1}\" is not a valid IP of type 000.000.000.000
.'})"
    );
    }
    //implement the ClientConverter's getClientScript
    public String getClientScript(FacesContext context,
                                  UIComponent component)
    {
      return null;
    }

    private LabeledFacesMessage _getMessage(UIComponent component,
String text)
    {
      // Using the LabeledFacesMessage allows the <tr:messages>
component to
      // properly prepend the label as a link.
      LabeledFacesMessage lfm =
        new LabeledFacesMessage(FacesMessage.SEVERITY_ERROR,
                                "Conversion Error", text);
      if (component != null)
      {
        Object label = null;
        label = component.getAttributes().get("label");
        if (label == null)
          label = component.getValueExpression("label");
        if (label != null)
          lfm.setLabel(label);
      }
      return lfm;
    }
}
```

3. Next we need to create a tag for this converter. For example, let's name this tag `converterIP`:

```
<tag>
  <name>convertIP</name>
  <tag-class>converterJSF.IPConverterTag</tag-class>
  <body-content>empty</body-content>
  <description>
      The convertIP tag converts a number to/from an IP address.
  </description>
</tag>
```

The `IPConverterTag` is as follows:

```
package converterJSF;
import javax.faces.application.Application;
import javax.faces.context.FacesContext;
import javax.faces.convert.Converter;
import javax.faces.webapp.ConverterELTag;
import javax.servlet.jsp.JspException;
public class IPConverterTag extends ConverterELTag
{
  public IPConverterTag()
  {
  }
  @Override
  protected Converter createConverter() throws JspException
  {
    Application app = FacesContext.getCurrentInstance().
getApplication();
    IPConverter converter = (IPConverter)app.createConverter(IPCon
verter.CONVERTER_ID);
    return converter;
  }
}
```

4. Call the converter from a JSP page, as shown next:

```
<tr:inputText value="#{ipBean.ip}"
  label="Insert a number of type 000000000000/000.000.000.000:">
  <trip:convertIP />
</tr:inputText>
```

How it works...

The submitted values are first evaluated by the JavaScript converter. As this converter runs on the client side, it can return potential errors almost immediately. If the submitted values successfully pass the JavaScript converter, then they arrive into the Java converter (on the server side) and after that in the backing bean. Reversing the process, the result values pass first through the Java converter and after that, through the JavaScript converter.

There's more...

Speaking about another release of Apache MyFaces you should know that Apache MyFaces Tomahawk project contains several custom objects that do not implement `UIComponent`. Some of these include objects that implement the `Converter` interface.

See also

The code bundled with this book contains a complete example of this recipe. The project can be opened with NetBeans 6.8 and is named: `Client_side_converters_with_Apache_Trinidad`.

2
Using Standard and Custom Validators in JSF

In this chapter, we will cover:

- ► Using a standard validator
- ► Customizing error messages for validators
- ► Creating a custom validator
- ► Binding validators to backing bean properties
- ► Validating forms with RichFaces `rich:beanValidator`
- ► Validating forms with RichFaces `rich:ajaxValidator`
- ► Apache MyFaces Commons validators
- ► Bean validation with `f:validateBean`
- ► Enforcing a value's presence with `f:validateRequired`
- ► Using regular expressions with `f:validateRegex`

Introduction

Validation ensures the application data contains the expected content. For example, we can validate the ranges of numbers or upper/lower limits, string lengths, date formats, and so on. Every time we need restrictions on a `UIInput` component or component whose classes extends `UIInput` we can use the validation mechanism. JSF provides four types of validation, as follows:

- Standard validation components
- Application-level validation
- Custom validation components
- Validation methods in backing beans

Validators are invoked during the `Process Validations Phase` of the JSF lifecycle. For example, if we assume a form that is submitted with a set of values, a validator for those values, a corresponding backing bean, and a render page, then the application lifecycle will be like this (notice when and where the validator is involved!):

- `Restore View Phase`: The backing bean is created and the components are stored into the `UIViewRoot`
- `Apply Request Values Phase`: The submitted values are decoded and set in the corresponding components in `UIViewRoot`
- `Process Validations Phase`: The validator is called and the submitted values are checked for the desired restrictions
- `Update Model Values Phase`: The validated values are set in the backing bean
- `Invoke Application Phase`: This phase is responsible for form processing
- `Render Response Phase`: The values that should be displayed are extracted from backing beans

Using the proper validator is the developer's choice. The developer is also responsible for customizing the error messages displayed when the validation fails. When the standard validators don't satisfy the application needs, the developer can write custom validators as you will see in our recipes.

Notice that our recipes make use of JSF 2.0 features, annotation, new navigation style, and no `faces-config.xml` file. Especially, you must notice the new JSF 2.0 validators described here.

But before that, let's start with a simple recipe about working with standard validators.

Using a standard validator

Using the standard JSF validators can be a simple task if you keep in mind two simple observations:

- ▸ They can be specified using a component's `validator` attribute or by nesting JSF-provided tags
- ▸ Validation can be performed only on `UIInput` components or components whose classes extend `UIInput`

In this recipe, you will see how to use the JSF standard validators listed next:

- ▸ `LengthValidator`: Counts the number of characters of a value and checks if it fits in a given range. The range boundaries are given by two attributes, as follows:
  - ❑ `minimum`: The minimum acceptable number of characters
  - ❑ `maximum`: The maximum acceptable number of characters
- ▸ `LongRangeValidator`: Attempts to convert the value to a number of Java `long` primitive type and checks to see if that number fits in a given range. The range boundaries are given by two attributes, as follows:
  - ❑ `minimum`: The minimum acceptable number
  - ❑ `maximum`: The maximum acceptable number

If these attributes are skipped, then the validator only checks if the value is numeric.

- ▸ `DoubleRangeValidator`: Attempts to convert the value to a number of Java `double` primitive type and checks to see if that number fits in a given range. The range boundaries are given by two attributes, as follows:
  - ❑ `minimum`: The minimum acceptable number
  - ❑ `maximum`: The maximum acceptable number

If these attributes are skipped, then the validator will only check if the value is numeric.

In this recipe, you will see how to use the first two previous validators.

Getting ready

We developed this recipe with NetBeans 6.8, JSF 2.0, and GlassFish v3. The JSF 2.0 classes were obtained from the NetBeans JSF 2.0 bundled library.

How to do it...

Let's suppose that we have a form with two fields representing a user's age and name. The age should be between 18 and 50 (we will apply the LongRangeValidator) and the name length will be between 5 and 25 characters (we will use the LengthValidator). Now, the corresponding form will look like this:

```
<h:form id="UserForm">
 <h:outputText value="Insert your age:"/><br />
 <h:inputText id="userAgeID" required="true"
            value="#{userBean.userAge}">
  <f:validateLongRange minimum="18" maximum="50"/>
 </h:inputText>
 <h:message showSummary="true" showDetail="false" for="userAgeID"
            style="color: red; text-decoration:overline"/>
 <br />
 <h:outputText value="Insert your first name:"/><br />
 <h:inputText id="userNameID" required="true"
            value="#{userBean.firstName}">
  <f:validateLength minimum="5" maximum="25" />
 </h:inputText>
 <h:message showSummary="true" showDetail="false" for="userNameID"
            style="color: red; text-decoration:overline"/>
 <br />

 <h:commandButton id="submit" action="response?faces-redirect=true"
                value="Submit"/>
</h:form>
```

How it works...

The mechanism is simple! Before populating the managed bean, the values are validated by the specified validators. If an error occurs while validating the values then the process returns an error message and displays the form again.

See also

The code bundled with this book contains a complete example of this recipe. The project can be opened with NetBeans 6.8 and it is named: Using_a_standard_validator.

Customizing error messages for validators

The error messages that are shown for each type of validation error are controlled by the `Message.properties` file, which is located in the `javax.faces` package of `jsf-api.jar`. You can customize/replace these error messages with your own or you can add new messages. Also, you can provide messages in different languages, not just in English. In this recipe, we will customize error messages using three scenarios, as follows:

- ▸ Customizing the default messages from `Message.properties`
- ▸ Creating our own error messages
- ▸ Generating error messages from custom converters

Getting ready

We developed this recipe with NetBeans 6.8, JSF 2.0, and GlassFish v3. The JSF 2.0 classes were obtained from the NetBeans JSF 2.0 bundled library.

How to do it...

Customizing the default messages from `Message.properties`—to accomplish this task we follow two simple steps. We start by creating our own properties file and copy into it the desired entries from `Messages.properties`. After that, we modify the entries accordingly to our needs (actually, we leave the property names as default and we modify their values). For example, we have created a properties file named `MyMessages.properties` as shown next:

```
javax.faces.component.UIInput.REQUIRED={0}: Value is required - custom
message.
javax.faces.validator.LongRangeValidator.NOT_IN_RANGE={2}: Specified
attribute is not between the expected values of {0} and {1} - custom
message.
javax.faces.validator.LengthValidator.MAXIMUM={1}: Value is greater
than allowable maximum of ''{0}''- custom message
javax.faces.validator.LengthValidator.MINIMUM={1}: Value is less than
allowable minimum of ''{0}''- custom message
```

Even if we are in JSF 2.0, we need to configure this properties file in `faces-config.xml`. This can be done as follows:

```
<application>
  <locale-config>
    <default-locale>en</default-locale>
  </locale-config>
  <message-bundle>users.MyMessages</message-bundle>
</application>
```

Going further, we create our own error message—in this case we can create our own property names in the properties file. For example, we have created the `MyMessages.properties` next (notice that this time we have a new set of entries—new property names and new values):

```
NOT_IN_RANGE=ERROR! - The inserted age is not between the accepted
interval, [18,50]!
NOT_IN_LENGTH=ERROR! - The inserted name must have a length between
5 and 25 characters!
AGE_REQUIRED=ERROR! - The age value is required!
NAME_REQUIRED=ERROR! - The name value is required!
```

Next we have to configure this properties file by following these steps:

1. In the corresponding page use the `f:loadBundle` tag to indicate the desired properties file (place this tag before the `<body>` tag of the page). For example:

    ```
    <f:loadBundle basename="users.MyMessages" var="msg"/>
    ```

2. Use the `requiredMessage` and `validatorMessage` attributes (notice that, in the same manner, for converters there is `converterMessage`) to indicate the corresponding error property name for each UI component. The `requiredMessage` attribute is used to indicate the error messages that should be displayed when no value was provided for the corresponding UI component (it can be a `String` or an EL expression and it has meaning when for the same UI component the `required` attribute is used and set to `true`). The `validatorMessage` attribute is used for indicating the error messages that should be displayed when the provided value can't be successfully validated (it can be a `String` or an EL expression). As per the example, let's suppose that we have a form with two fields representing a user's age and name. The age should be between `18` and `50` (we will apply the `LongRangeValidator`) and the name length will be between `5` and `25` characters (we will use the `LengthValidator`). The error messages will be provided by our `MyMessages.properties`. For this we have the following code:

    ```
    <h:head>
      <title>Customize messages for validators</title>
    </h:head>
    <f:loadBundle basename="users.MyMessages" var="msg"/>
    <h:body>
     <h:form id="UserForm">
      <h:outputText value="Insert your age:"/><br />
      <h:inputText id="userAgeID" required="true"
                   value="#{userBean.userAge}"
                   requiredMessage="#{msg.AGE_REQUIRED}"
                   validatorMessage="#{msg.NOT_IN_RANGE}">
       <f:validateLongRange minimum="18" maximum="50"/>
      </h:inputText>
    ```

```
<h:message showSummary="true" showDetail="false" for="userAgeID"
           style="color: red; text-decoration:overline"/>
<br />
<h:outputText value="Insert your first name:"/><br />
<h:inputText id="userNameID" required="true"
             value="#{userBean.firstName}"
             requiredMessage="#{msg.NAME_REQUIRED}"
             validatorMessage="#{msg.NOT_IN_LENGTH}">
 <f:validateLength minimum="5" maximum="25" />
</h:inputText>
<h:message showSummary="true" showDetail="false"
           for="userNameID"
           style="color: red; text-decoration:overline"/>
<br />
<h:commandButton id="submit"
                 action="response?faces-redirect=true"
                 value="Submit"/>
</h:form>
</h:body>
```

3. Configure this properties file in the `faces-config.xml`. This can be done as shown next:

```
<application>
  <locale-config>
    <default-locale>en</default-locale>
  </locale-config>
  <message-bundle>users.MyMessages</message-bundle>
</application>
```

> Notice that even if we are using JSF 2.0, we still need the `faces-config.xml` file. Annotations and the implicit navigation allow us to write an application without needing a `faces-config.xml` fille. but there are still cases where the configuration file is needed. Localization information, advanced features such as `ELResolvers`, `PhaseListeners`, or artifacts that rely on the decorator pattern still require a `faces-config.xml` file.

How it works...

The main key resides in the configuration made in `faces-config.xml`. It indicates to JSF that the corresponding error messages should be found in the specified properties file instead of the default one. When the custom properties' names override the default ones, JSF will automatically detect them. When the properties' names are totally new, you can use the `requiredMessage` and `validatorMessage` to fit them accordingly to the UI components. Finally, note that the message aspect is customizable through the `h:message` tag. This tag is related to its UI component through the `for` attribute, which has the same value as the `id` attribute of the UI component.

There's more...

In the case of custom converters you can programmatically generate custom errors like this:

```
FacesMessage message = new FacesMessage();
            message.setDetail("error details");
            message.setSummary("error summary");
            message.setSeverity(FacesMessage.SEVERITY_ERROR);
      throw new ValidatorException(message);
```

See also

The code bundled with this book contains a complete example of this recipe. The project can be opened with NetBeans 6.8 and it is named:

- `Customize_error_messages_for_validators_1`
- `Customize_error_messages_for_validators_2`

Creating a custom validator

When standard validators don't satisfy your application needs, you need to write a custom validator. As per example, in this recipe you will see how to validate an IP address, an e-mail address, and a zip code. Following this strategy, you can write custom validators for phone numbers, credit card numbers, fax numbers, and so on.

Getting ready

We developed this recipe with NetBeans 6.8, JSF 2.0, and GlassFish v3. The JSF 2.0 classes were obtained from the NetBeans JSF 2.0 bundled library.

How to do it...

Writing custom validators is a straightforward process that starts with the task of creating a class that implements the `javax.faces.validator.Validator` interface and the `validate` method.

For JSF 1.2, register your custom validator in the `faces-confix.xml` file. For JSF 2.0 use the `javax.faces.validator.FacesValidator` annotation.

After we have written the validator class, we call it from JSF pages through the `<f:validator/>` tag.

As per example, we have developed a custom validator to validate an IP address as shown next:

```java
import java.util.regex.Matcher;
import java.util.regex.Pattern;
import javax.faces.application.FacesMessage;
import javax.faces.component.UIComponent;
import javax.faces.context.FacesContext;
import javax.faces.validator.FacesValidator;
import javax.faces.validator.Validator;
import javax.faces.validator.ValidatorException;

@FacesValidator(value = "ipValidator")
public class IpValidator implements Validator {

    private static final String IP_REGEX = "^([1-9]|[1-9][0-9]|1[0-
9][0-9]|2[0-4][0-9]|25[0-5])(\\.([0-9]|[1-9][0-9]|1[0-9][0-9]|2[0-
4][0-9]|25[0-5])){3}$";

    public void validate(FacesContext context, UIComponent component,
Object value) throws ValidatorException {

        String ipAddress = (String) value;
        Pattern mask = null;

        mask = Pattern.compile(IP_REGEX);
        Matcher matcher = mask.matcher(ipAddress);

        if (!matcher.matches()) {
```

```
          FacesMessage message = new FacesMessage();
          message.setDetail("IP not valid");
          message.setSummary("IP not valid");
          message.setSeverity(FacesMessage.SEVERITY_ERROR);
          throw new ValidatorException(message);
        }
      }
    }
```

And we have called this custom validator like this:

```
<h:inputText id="ipID" required="true" value="#{ipBean.ipValue}">
    <f:validator validatorId="ipValidator"/>
</h:inputText>
```

How it works...

It works exactly like a standard validator, but this time the called validator is a custom one. Before populating the managed bean, the values are validated by the custom validator. If an error occurs while validating the values then the process returns an error message and re-displays the form.

There's more...

Since regular expressions are often used in validators, here it is a short list of the most used:

- E-mail: `^[\\w\\-]([\\.\\w])+[\\w]+@([\\w\\-]+\\.)+[A-Z]{2,4}$`
- City abbreviation: `.*, [A-Z][A-Z]`
- Social security number, such as `###-##-####`: `[0-9]\{3\}-[0-9]\{2\}-[0-9]\{4\}`
- Date, in numeric format, such as 2003-08-06: `[0-9]\{4\}-[0-9]\{2\}-[0-9]\{2\}`

See also

The code bundled with this book contains a complete example of this recipe. The project can be opened with NetBeans 6.8 and it is named: `Creating_a_custom_validator`.

Binding validators to backing bean properties

JSF standard validator tags allow the `binding` attribute (this is also true for listener and converter tags). This means that developers can bind validator implementations to backing bean properties. The main advantages of using the binding facility are:

▸ The developer can allow to the backing bean to instantiate the implementation

▸ The backing bean can programmatically access the implementation's attributes

Getting ready

We developed this recipe with NetBeans 6.8, JSF 2.0, and GlassFish v3. The JSF 2.0 classes were obtained from the NetBeans JSF 2.0 bundled library.

How to do it...

To successfully accomplish a binding task, you can follow three simple steps (these steps are true for converter, listener, and validator tags):

1. Nest the validator (listener, converter) tag in the component tag.
2. Put in the backing bean a property that takes and return the validator (listener, converter) implementation class.
3. Reference the backing bean property using a value expression from the `binding` attribute of the validator (listener, converter) tag.

As per the example, let's bind the standard `f:validateLongRange` validator to a backing bean property. The idea is to let the backing bean set the values for the `minimum` and `maximum` attributes. First, you have to register the validator onto the component by nesting the `f:validateLongRange` tag within the component tag. Then, you have to reference the property with the `binding` attribute of the `f:validateLongRange` tag.

```
<h:form id="IpForm">
  <h:outputText value="Insert your age:"/><br />
  <h:inputText id="ageID" required="true"
             value="#{userBean.userAge}">
    <f:validateLongRange binding="#{userBean.longAge}"/>
  </h:inputText>
  <h:message showSummary="true" showDetail="false" for="ageID"
           style="color: red; text-decoration:overline"/>
  <br />

  <h:commandButton id="submit" action="response?faces-redirect=true"
                 value="Submit"/>
</h:form>
```

The `longAge` property is defined in the following managed bean:

```
package users;

import javax.faces.bean.ManagedBean;
import javax.faces.bean.SessionScoped;
import javax.faces.validator.LongRangeValidator;

@ManagedBean
@SessionScoped
public class UserBean {

  private int userAge;
  private LongRangeValidator longAge;

  public int getUserAge(){
    return this.userAge;
  }

  public void setUserAge(int userAge){
    this.userAge=userAge;
  }

  public LongRangeValidator getLongAge(){
    return this.longAge;
  }

  public void setLongAge(LongRangeValidator longAge){
    longAge.setMinimum(18);
    longAge.setMaximum(90);
    this.longAge=longAge;
  }

}
```

How it works...

In our example, the backing bean sets the `minimum` and `maximum` values within the `f:validateLongRange` tag, which means that the user's input will be constrained by these boundaries. This time the number's range is indicated without using specific attributes in `f:validateLongRange` tag. Instead of this, we use the `binding` attribute to reference the `longAge` property, which is a `LongRangeValidator` instance, offering us access to this class's methods.

See also

The code bundled with this book contains a complete example of this recipe. The project can be opened with NetBeans 6.8 and it is named: `Bind_validators_to_backing_bean_ properties`.

Validating forms with RichFaces rich:beanValidator

The `rich:beanValidator` is a component designed to provide validation using Hibernate Validator model-based constraints (details about Hibernate Validator can be found at `https://www.hibernate.org/412.html`). In this recipe, we will validate a simple form made up of two fields representing the e-mail address and age of a user.

Getting ready

We developed this recipe with NetBeans 6.8, JSF 2.0, and GlassFish v3. The JSF 2.0 classes were obtained from the NetBeans JSF 2.0 bundled library. In addition, we have used RichFaces 3.3.3.BETA1, which provides support for JSF 2.0. You can download this distribution from `http://www.jboss.org/richfaces`. The RichFaces libraries (including necessary dependencies) are in the book code bundle, under the `/JSF_libs/RichFaces – JSF 2.0` folder.

How to do it...

The `rich:beanValidator` tag is usually nested in a UI Component, like `h:inputText`. Next, you can see an example (notice that the `summary` attribute will contain details displayed about the validation error):

```
<h:form id="form">
  <h:panelGrid columns="3">
    <h:outputLabel for="email" value="Email Address:" />
    <h:inputText id="email" value="#{bean.email}" label="Email">
     <rich:beanValidator summary="Invalid Email address"/>
    </h:inputText>
  <rich:message for="email"/>
  <h:outputLabel for="age" value="Age:" />
  <h:inputText id="age" value="#{bean.age}" label="Age">
   <rich:beanValidator
       summary="Invalid age, must be between 18 and 90"/>
  </h:inputText>
```

```
    <rich:message for="age"/>
  </h:panelGrid>
  <h:commandButton value="Submit"></h:commandButton>
  <rich:messages/>
</h:form>
```

The validator restrictions are specified in Hibernate style using the corresponding annotations in a bean. In our example, the `Bean` bean can be seen next:

```
package bean;

import org.hibernate.validator.Email;
import org.hibernate.validator.Range;
import org.hibernate.validator.NotEmpty;

public class Bean {

  private String email;
  private Integer age;

  @Range(min=18, max=90)
  public Integer getAge() {
    return age;
  }

  public void setAge(Integer age) {
    this.age = age;
  }

  @NotEmpty
  @Email
  public String getEmail() {
    return email;
  }

  public void setEmail(String email) {
    this.email = email;
  }
}
```

For more Hibernate validators check the `org.hibernate.validator` package. In our example, we have used the `@Email`, `@NotEmpty`, and `@Range` validators.

How it works...

It works like a common validator, but this time the validator restrictions are taken directly from the bean, instead of using dedicated attributes inside the validator tag.

There's more...

Another important validator from RichFaces is the `rich:graphValidator`. The `rich:graphValidator` component is much like `rich:beanValidator`. The difference between these two components is that in order to validate some input data with a `rich:beanValidator` component, it should be a nested element of an input component, whereas `rich:graphValidator` wraps multiple input components and validates the data received from them.

See also

The code bundled with this book contains a complete example of this recipe. The project can be opened with NetBeans 6.8 and it is named: `Validate_forms_with_RichFaces_ BeanValidator`.

Validating forms with RichFaces rich:ajaxValidator

The `rich:ajaxValidator` is a component designed to provide validation using Hibernate model-based constraints and AJAX mechanism (details about Hibernate Validator can be found at `https://www.hibernate.org/412.html`). In this recipe, we will validate a simple form made of two fields representing the e-mail address and age of a user.

Getting ready

We developed this recipe with NetBeans 6.8, JSF 2.0, and GlassFish v3. The JSF 2.0 classes were obtained from the NetBeans JSF 2.0 bundled library. In addition, we have used RichFaces 3.3.3.BETA1, which provide support for JSF 2.0. You can download this distribution from `http://www.jboss.org/richfaces`. The RichFaces libraries (including necessary dependencies) are in the book code bundle, under the `/JSF_libs/RichFaces – JSF 2.0` folder.

How to do it...

The `rich:ajaxValidator` tag is usually nested in a UI Component, such as `h:inputText`. The most important attribute of this tag is the `event` attribute. Its value indicates the event that should happen before the validation takes place. As per the example, the `onkeyup` event will validate the corresponding input every time a key is pressed and released (this is possible thanks to the AJAX mechanism). Here is an example:

```
<h:form id="form">
  <h:panelGrid columns="3">
    <h:outputLabel for="email" value="Email Address:" />
    <h:inputText id="email" value="#{bean.email}" label="Email">
      <rich:ajaxValidator event="onkeyup"
                          summary="Invalid Email address"/>
    </h:inputText>
    <rich:message for="email"/>
    <h:outputLabel for="age" value="Age:" />
    <h:inputText id="age" value="#{bean.age}" label="Age">
      <rich:ajaxValidator event="onkeyup"
                  summary="Invalid age, must be between 18 and 90"/>
    </h:inputText>
    <rich:message for="age"/>
  </h:panelGrid>
  <h:commandButton value="Submit"></h:commandButton>
  <rich:messages/>
</h:form>
```

The validator restrictions are specified in Hibernate validator style using the corresponding annotations in a bean. In our example, the `Bean` bean is the one from listing `Bean.java`, in the previous recipe.

How it works...

This time the validator restrictions are taken directly from the bean, instead of using dedicated attributes inside the validator tag. In addition, the AJAX mechanism allows JSF to accomplish the validation tasks without submitting the form.

See also

The code bundled with this book contains a complete example of this recipe. The project can be opened with NetBeans 6.8 and it is named: `Validate_forms_with_RichFaces_ajaxValidator`.

Apache MyFaces Commons validators

The Apache MyFaces Commons project contains a set of validators (`myfaces-validators`), converters (`myfaces-converters`), and utils (`myfaces-commons-utils`). These are JARs that can be used with any JSF framework.

In this recipe, we are using validators. The most widely used validators are:

- `<mcv:validateCSV>`
- `<mcv:validateCompareTo>`
- `<mcv:validateCreditCard>`
- `<mcv:validateDateRestriction>`
- `<mcv:validateEmail>`
- `<mcv:validateISBN>`
- `<mcv:validateRegExpr>`
- `<mcv:validateUrl>`

In this recipe you will see how to use the `mcv:validateEmail` validator. Based on this example, it will be simple to work with the rest of the validators.

Getting ready

We developed this recipe with NetBeans 6.8, JSF 2.0, and GlassFish v3. The JSF 2.0 classes were obtained from the NetBeans JSF 2.0 bundled library. In addition, we have used Apache MyFaces Commons 1.2, which is designed for JSF 1.2, but it seems that it supports JSF 2.0 also (as far as we have tested it, no problems occurred). You can download this distribution from `http://myfaces.apache.org/commons/download.html`. The Apache MyFaces Commons libraries (including necessary dependencies) are in the book code bundle, under the `/JSF_libs/Apache MyFaces Commons – JSF 2.0` folder.

How to do it...

First you have to provide access to the Apache MyFaces Commons library. Knowing that this library has the namespace `http://myfaces.apache.org/commons/validators` and the most used prefix is `mcv`, you can accomplish this task as shown next:

```
<%@taglib prefix="mcv" uri="http://myfaces.apache.org/commons/
validators"%>
```

Next you can nest the corresponding validator inside an input tag, as shown next:

```
<h:inputText id="email1" value="#{user.email}" required="true">
 <mcv:validateEmail/>
</h:inputText>
<h:message for="email1"/>
```

How it works...

Apache MyFaces Commons validators follow the same pattern as an standard JSF converters. In practice, they are an extension of JSF validators, which means that you can do with them exactly what you can do with a JSF Core validator.

See also

The code bundled with this book contains a complete example of this recipe. The project can be opened with NetBeans 6.8 and it is named: `Apache_MyFaces_Commons_Validators`.

More details are available at:

`http://myfaces.apache.org/commons12/myfaces-validators12/index.html`

`http://myfaces.apache.org/commons/index.html`

Bean validation with f:validateBean

Probably the most important validation tag provided by JSF 2.0 is the `f:validateBean` tag. For a start, you have to know that this tag is part of a mechanism whose aim is to integrate Bean Validation with JSF 2.0. Bean Validation—known as JSR 303 (`http://jcp.org/en/jsr/detail?id=303`); officially part of the new Java EE 6 this defines a metadata model and API for JavaBean validation. The default "metadata source is annotations, with the ability to override and extend the meta-data through the use of XML validation descriptors". In this recipe, you will see how to exploit the Bean Validation.

Getting ready

We developed this recipe with NetBeans 6.8, JSF 2.0, and GlassFish v3. The JSF 2.0 classes were obtained from the NetBeans JSF 2.0 bundled library.

How to do it...

Instead of placing validation rules in different layers of the application and keeping them synchronized, we can take use of Bean Validation and use its constraint annotations in the managed beans—JSF 2 provides built-in integration with JSR-303 constraints—as in the following example:

```
public class userBean {

@NotEmpty(message = "The name cannot be empty!")
@Size(min = 5, max = 20, message="You must provide a name between 5
                            and 20 characters!")
private String name;

@Digits(integer = 2, fraction = 0, message = "You must provide a
                                    valid age!")
@Range(min=18, max=99, message="You must be over 18 years old!")
private int age;

@NotEmpty(message = "The email cannot be empty!")
//instead of @Pattern you can use @Email
@Pattern(regexp =
            "[a-zA-Z0-9_]*[@]{1}[a-zA-Z0-9_]*[.]{1}[a-zA-Z]{2,3}",
        message="You must provide at least
                an well-formed e-mail address!")
private String email;
...
```

In the following table you can see a summary of the Bean Validation annotation with a short description:

Annotation	BVS *	Apply on	Use
@AssertFalse	Yes	Field/property	Check that the annotated element is false.
@AssertTrue	Yes	Field/property	Check that the annotated element is true.
@DecimalMax	Yes	Field/property Supported types are: BigDecimal, BigInteger, String, byte, short, int, and long.	Check that the annotated element is a number whose value is lower than or equal to the specified maximum.

Annotation	BVS *	Apply on	Use
`@DecimalMin`	Yes	Field/property Supported types are: `BigDecimal, BigInteger, String, byte, short, int, long.`	Check that the annotated element is a number whose value is higher than or equal to the specified minmum.
`@Digits(integer=, fraction=)`	Yes	Field/property Supported types are: `BigDecimal, BigInteger, String, byte, short, int, long.`	Check that the annotated element is a number having up to `integer` digits and `fraction` fractional digits.
`@Future`	Yes	Field/property Supported types are `java.util.Date` and `java.util.Calendar.`	Check that the annotated date is in the future.
`@Max`	Yes	Field/property Supported types are: `BigDecimal, BigInteger, String, byte, short, int, long.`	Check that the annotated value is less than or equal to the specified maximum.
`@Min`	Yes	Field/property Supported types are: `BigDecimal, BigInteger, String, byte, short, int, long.`	Check that the annotated value is higher than or equal to the specified minimum.
`@NotNull`	Yes	Field/property	Check that the annotated value is not null.
`@Null`	Yes	Field/property	Check that the annotated value is null.
`@Valid`	Yes	Field/property	Perform validation recursively on the associated object.
`@Past`	Yes	Field/property Supported types are `java.util.Date` and `java.util.Calendar.`	Check that the annotated date is in the past.

Annotation	BVS *	Apply on	Use
`@Size(min=, max=)`	Yes	field/property Supported types are `String`, `Collection`, `Map`, and `arrays`.	Check if the annotated element size is between `min` and `max` (inclusive).
`@Length(min=, max=)`	No	Field/property	Check that the annotated string is between `min` and `max` included.
`@NotEmpty`	No	Field/property	Check that the annotated string is not null or empty.
`@Email`	No	Field/property	Check that the annotated string is a valid email address.
`@Range(min=, max=)`	No	Field/property Supported types are: `BigDecimal`, `BigInteger`, `String`, `byte,\ short`, `int`, and `long`.	Check that the annotated value lies between the specified minimum and maximum (inclusive).

* BVS - Bean Validation Specification

The annotations marked as "yes" belong to BVS and they can be found in the `javax.validation.constraints` package, while the ones marked with "no" can be found in the `org.hibernate.validator.constraints` package.

After we set our annotation, we can control (fine tune) the validation from the JSF pages with the `f:validateBean` tag. The `f:validateBean` supports the following optional attributes:

- `binding`: A `ValueExpression` that evaluates to an object that implements `javax.faces.validate.BeanValidator`.

- `disabled`: A boolean value enabling page-level determination of whether or not this validator is enabled on the enclosing component.

- `validationGroups`: A comma-delimited string of type-safe validation groups that are passed to the Bean Validation API when validating the value.

▸ By default, the Bean Validator is enabled, therefore our JSF pages may not contain any code fragments that reveal the presence of the Bean Validator. For example, the following JSF page makes use of Bean Validator without our explicit specification:

```
...
<h:form>
 <h:panelGrid columns="2">
  <h:outputText value="Name:"/>
  <h:inputText value="#{userBean.name}"/>
  <h:outputText value="Age:"/>
  <h:inputText value="#{userBean.age}"/>
  <h:outputText value="E-mail:"/>
  <h:inputText value="#{userBean.email}"/>
 </h:panelGrid>
 <h:commandButton value="Submit" action="index?faces-
 redirect=true"/>
</h:form>
...
```

A possible output is in the following screenshot:

Now, if we want to disable the Bean Validator for a specific field, then we must get involved and set the `disabled` attribute to `false`, as in the following code, where we disable validation for the user age:

```
...
<h:outputText value="Age:"/>
<h:inputText value="#{userBean.age}">
 <f:validateBean disabled="true" />
</h:inputText>
...
```

Add a `context-param` to your `web.xml`, `javax.faces.VALIDATE_EMPTY_FIELDS`, by default it is set to `auto`. If it is `true`, all submitted fields will be validated. This is necessary to delegate validation of whether a field can be null/empty to the model validator. If it is `false`, empty values will not be passed to the validators. If it is `auto`, the default will be `true` only if Bean Validation is in the environment, `false` otherwise (which keeps backward compatibility).

There's more...

You also may want to save the validation groups—allowing you to restrict the set of constraints applied during validation—in an attribute on the parent to be used as defaults inherited by any Bean Validator in that context (an empty `String` is not allowed). If no validation groups are inherited, assume the `Default` validation group, `javax.validation.groups.Default`.

The property `validationGroups` on BeanValidator is used to allow the view designer to specify a comma-separated list of groups that should be validated. A group is represented by the fully qualified class name of its interface. If the `validationGroups` attribute is omitted, the `Default` (`javax.validation.groups.Default`) group will be used. If the model validator is set as the default validator, this tag can be used to specify validation groups for this input.

In practice, groups are just simple Java interfaces. Using interfaces makes the usage of groups type safe and allows for easy refactoring. In addition, groups can inherit from each other via class inheritance. As per the example, we can use two different groups as shown next:

```
//the usersIdsGroup
public interface usersIdsGroup {
}

//the usersCredentialsGroup
public interface usersCredentialsGroup {
}
```

Next, we can bind managed beans' properties to groups as shown next:

```
...
@NotEmpty(message = "The name cannot be empty!",
        groups = beans.usersIdsGroup.class)
@Size(min = 5, max = 20, message = "You must provide a name between 5
and 20 characters!", groups = beans.usersIdsGroup.class)
private String name;

@Digits(integer = 2, fraction = 0,
        message = "You must provide a valid age!",
```

```
                groups = beans.usersIdsGroup.class)
@Range(min = 18, max = 99,
        message = "You must be over 18 years old!",
        groups = beans.usersIdsGroup.class)
private int age;

@NotEmpty(message = "The email cannot be empty!",
          groups = beans.usersIdsGroup.class)
//instead of @Pattern you can use @Email
@Pattern(
        regexp = "[a-zA-Z0-9_]*[@]{1}[a-zA-Z0-9_]*[.]{1}[a-zA-Z]{2,3}",
        message = "You must provide at least an well-formed e-mail
                   address!",
        groups = beans.usersIdsGroup.class)
   private String email;

@NotEmpty(message = "The ID cannot be empty!",
          groups = beans.usersCredentialsGroup.class)
  @Size(min = 5, max = 20,
        message = "You must provide an ID between 5 and 20
                   characters!",
        groups = beans.usersCredentialsGroup.class)
private String nickname;

@NotEmpty(message = "The password cannot be empty!",
          groups = beans.usersCredentialsGroup.class)
@Size(min = 5, max = 20,
    message = "You must provide a password between 5 and 20
               characters!",
     groups = beans.usersCredentialsGroup.class)
private String password;
...
```

As you can see, the `name`, `age`, and `email` properties belong to the `usersIdsGroup` group, while the `nickname` and `password` properties belongs to the `usersCredentialsGroup` group. Next, in a JSF page, we can validate both groups like this:

```
...
<f:validateBean validationGroups="beans.usersIdsGroup,usersCredential
sGroup">

   <h:outputText value="Name:"/>
   <h:inputText value="#{userBean.name}"/>
   <h:outputText value="Age:"/>
   <h:inputText value="#{userBean.age}"/>
```

```
    <h:outputText value="E-mail:"/>
    <h:inputText value="#{userBean.email}"/>

    <h:outputText value="ID:"/>
    <h:inputText value="#{userBean.nickname}"/>
    <h:outputText value="Password"/>
    <h:inputSecret value="#{userBean.password}"/>
</f:validateBean>
...
```

If we want to validate only the `usersIdsGroup` group, then we remove this group from the value of the `validationGroups` attribute:

```
...
<f:validateBean validationGroups="beans.usersIdsGroup">
...
</f:validateBean>
...
```

You also may call a Bean validator programatically. The following code snippet shows you how to accomplish this:

```
public class UserValidator {

public boolean validateUser(userBean user) {

  ValidatorFactory factory =
  Validation.buildDefaultValidatorFactory();
  Validator validator = factory.getValidator();

  Set<ConstraintViolation<userBean>> constraintViolations =
    validator.validate(user, Default.class);

  if (!constraintViolations.isEmpty())
     return false;

  constraintViolations = validator.validate(user,
                                      beans.usersIdsGroup.class);

  return constraintViolations.isEmpty();
  }
}
```

How it works...

As you just saw, Bean Validation centralized constraint declarations and is based on a several standard constraint annotations (for example `@Size`, `@Min`, `@Max`, `@AssertTrue`, `@AssertFalse`, and so on) and also allows custom constraints to be defined. In addition we can use groups that allow us to restrict the set of constraints applied during validation. This time the validator restrictions are taken directly from the bean, instead of using dedicated attributes inside the validator tag.

The complete reference for Bean Validation is JSR-303 available at `http://jcp.org/en/jsr/detail?id=303`.

See also

The code bundled with this book contains a complete example of this recipe. The project can be opened with NetBeans 6.8 and it is named: `Bean_validation_with_validateBean_1` and `Bean_validation_with_validateBean_2`.

More details about the `f:validateBean` tag specification can be found at:

`https://javaserverfaces.dev.java.net/nonav/docs/2.0/pdldocs/facelets/f/validateBean.html`

Enforcing a value's presence with f:validateRequired

Starting with JSF 2.0, a new set of validators is available. One of these is the `f:validateRequired`, which is a validator used to enforce the presence of a value. In practice, its effect is the same as the `required` attribute set to `true` on a `UIInput` component. In this recipe, you will see an example of using this new validator.

Getting ready

We developed this recipe with NetBeans 6.8, JSF 2.0, and GlassFish v3. The JSF 2.0 classes were obtained from the NetBeans JSF 2.0 bundled library.

How to do it...

The following example will make things clear in a few seconds. We assume a `UIInput` component used for grabbing an e-mail address from the user. Since we want to enforce the necessity of this e-mail address we can use `f:validateRequired`, as shown next:

```
...
<h:form>
  <h:outputText value="E-mail:"/>
  <h:inputText value="#{emailBean.email}"
               validatorMessage="You must provide an e-mail of type
                                myemail@domain.com!">
    <f:validateRequired/>
  </h:inputText>
  <h:commandButton value="Submit"
                   action="index?faces-redirect=true"/>
</h:form>
...
```

How it works...

As we said earlier, it works like the `required` attribute set it to `true` on a `UIInput` component. As per the example, the following code does the same thing, without using the `f:validateRequired`:

```
...
<h:form>
  <h:outputText value="E-mail:"/>
  <h:inputText value="#{emailBean.email}" required="true"
               requiredMessage="You must provide an e-mail of type
                                myemail@domain.com!" />
  <h:commandButton value="Submit"
                   action="index?faces-redirect=true"/>
</h:form>
...
```

See also

The code bundled with this book contains a complete example of this recipe. The project can be opened with NetBeans 6.8 and it is named: `validateRequired_and_validateRegex_tags`.

More details about the `f:validateRequired` tag specification can be found at `https://javaserverfaces.dev.java.net/nonav/docs/2.0/pdldocs/facelets/f/validateRequired.html`

Using regular expressions with f:validateRegex

Another validator available starting with JSF 2.0 is `f:validateRegex`. This validator uses the `pattern` attribute to validate the wrapping component. The value of `pattern` is provided as a Java regular expression. In this recipe, you will see how to use this validator to validate an e-mail address against the proper regular expression.

Getting ready

We developed this recipe with NetBeans 6.8, JSF 2.0, and GlassFish v3. The JSF 2.0 classes were obtained from the NetBeans JSF 2.0 bundled library.

How to do it...

The following code snippet validates the value provided into a `UIInput` component as an e-mail address value:

```
...
<h:form>
  <h:outputText value="E-mail:"/>
  <h:inputText value="#{emailBean.email}"
               validatorMessage="You must provide an e-mail of type
                                 myemail@domain.com!">
    <f:validateRegex pattern=
          "[a-zA-Z0-9_]*[@]{1}[a-zA-Z0-9_]*[.]{1}[a-zA-Z]{2,3}" />
  </h:inputText>

  <h:commandButton value="Submit" action=
                                "index?faces-redirect=true"/>
</h:form>
...
```

How it works...

The `f:validateRegex` works exactly as expected—the entire pattern is matched against the provided `String` value of the component. If it matches, it's valid, otherwise a validation error message is returned.

See also

The code bundled with this book contains a complete example of this recipe. The project can be opened with NetBeans 6.8 and it is named: `validateRequired_and_validateRegex_tags`.

More details about the `f:validateReqex` tag specification can be found at `https://javaserverfaces.dev.java.net/nonav/docs/2.0/pdldocs/facelets/f/validateRegex.html`.

3
Security

In this chapter, we will cover:

- ▸ Working with the JSF Security project
- ▸ Using the JSF Security project without JAAS Roles
- ▸ Using secured managed beans with JSF Security
- ▸ Using Acegi/Spring security in JSF applications

Introduction

Security—there is only one reason to use it and many other reasons to not. In other words, protect your websites against malicious attacks, but get a bigger, slower, and more expensive final product.

In this chapter, you will see a series of four recipes for increasing the security of your JSF applications. You will see how to use the JSF Security project, how to manage JAAS roles and the JSF Security layer, and how to use Acegi/Spring security for writing a login application.

Working with the JSF Security project

JSF Security is a set of security extensions for JavaServer Faces to solve common access control problems. JSF Security acts like a security layer by extending the JSF EL (**Expression Language**). Basically, it works in a separate scope, named `securityScope`, and accesses the security artifacts through EL language. In this recipe, you will see how to use the EL extensions provided by the JSF Security project.

Getting ready

We have developed this recipe with NetBeans 6.8, JSF 2.0, and GlassFish v3. The JSF 2.0 classes were obtained from the NetBeans JSF 2.0 bundled library. In addition, we have used JSF Security 1.0, which provides support for JSF 2.0. You can download this distribution from `http://sourceforge.net/projects/jsf-security/files/jsf-security/`. The jsf-security libraries (including necessary dependencies) are in the book code bundle, under the `/JSF_libs/jsf-security - JSF 2.0` folder. The JSF Security project is available in ZIP format. All you have to do is to add the `jsf-security.jar` archive to your JSF projects.

How to do it...

Before developing an effective application let's see the available EL expressions:

Expression	Effect
`#{securityScope.authType}`	The authentication type being used; with container security this will be `BASIC`, `FORM`, `DIGEST`, or JAAS may return custom strings.
`#{securityScope.remoteUser}`	The user name of the authenticated user.
`#{securityScope.securityEnabled}`	If security is currently enabled this EL returns `true`. It returns `false` if no security is installed or the user is not yet authenticated.
`#{securityScope.userInRole['role_1, role_2, … role_n']}`	This returns `true` if the user is in at least one of the roles. It returns `false` if the user is not in any of the roles or if the user is not currently authenticated.
`#{securityScope.userInAllRoles['role_1, role_2, … role_n']}`	This returns `true` if the user is in all of the roles. It returns `false` if the user is not in all of the roles, or if the user is not currently authenticated.

Next, we will write a JSF page that will put the previous expressions in a single example. Assuming that we already have a role named, `JSP-ROLE`, our page looks as shown next:

```
<%@page contentType="text/html" pageEncoding="UTF-8"%>

<%@taglib prefix="f" uri="http://java.sun.com/jsf/core"%>
<%@taglib prefix="h" uri="http://java.sun.com/jsf/html"%>
```

```
<!DOCTYPE HTML PUBLIC "-//W3C//DTD HTML 4.01 Transitional//EN"
    "http://www.w3.org/TR/html4/loose.dtd">

<f:view>
 <html>
  <head>
   <meta http-equiv="Content-Type" content="text/html;
         charset=UTF-8"/>
   <title>JSF-SECURITY</title>
  </head>
  <body>
   <h:form>
    <h:panelGroup rendered="#{!securityScope.securityEnabled}">
     <h:outputText value="Security is not enabled..."/>
    </h:panelGroup>
    <h:panelGrid columns="2"
                 rendered="#{securityScope.securityEnabled}">
     <h:outputText value="Remote User"/>
     <h:outputText value="#{securityScope.remoteUser}"/>
     <h:outputText value="Auth Type"/>
     <h:outputText value="#{securityScope.authType}"/>
     <h:outputText value="User in JSP-ROLE "/>
     <h:outputText value="#{securityScope.userInRole['JSP-ROLE']}"/>
     <h:outputText value="User in all of JSP-ROLE "/>
     <h:outputText value="#{securityScope.userInAllRoles['JSP
                                                    -ROLE']}"/>
    </h:panelGrid>
   </h:form>
  </body>
 </html>
</f:view>
```

The `jsf_security.jar` contains a `faces-config.xml` file in its `META-INF` directory. This defines custom `<variable-resolver>` and `<property-resolver>` values, as shown next:

```
<application>
 <property-resolver>
  com.groundside.jsf.securityresolver.SecurityPropertyResolver
 </property-resolver>
 <variable-resolver>
   com.groundside.jsf.securityresolver.SecurityVariableResolver
 </variable-resolver>
</application>
```

The JSP-ROLE was configured under Sun GlassFish Enterprise Server V3 Prelude container, but you can set it on any other container using the right knowledge. For more details of how to configure the JSP-ROLE under GlassFish you can try http://www.informit.com/authors/bio.aspx?a=3064cf95-43af-48f6-9303-8d2fdd7f3706.

The output of this example is in the following screenshot (we set the BASIC authentication type in the web.xml descriptor):

How it works...

The JSF Security layer interacts with the default security layers and provides EL extensions for managing common access control problems. The extensions are completely pluggable and can adapt to more or less any mechanism that is used for authentication and authorization that the programmer can reach from the FacesContext/Request/Session.

Notice that, by default JSF Security hooks into J2EE container-managed security using the J2EEContainerSecurityAttributeResolver. It is possible to plug in an alternative implementation here by a simple configuration change.

See also

The code bundled with this book contains a complete example of this recipe. The project can be opened with NetBeans 6.8 and it is named: Working_with_jsf_security_project.

Using the JSF Security project without JAAS Roles

In the default implementation of the JSF Security project (see the recipe *Working with the JSF Security project*), the application uses a JAAS implementation for the authentication and authorization. In this recipe, we will modify the JSF Security project to use roles stored in a database, and also those that are added to the HttpSession context depending on choices made by the user in our application.

Getting ready

Refer to the previous recipe.

How to do it...

After you have downloaded the JSF Security project, follow the given steps:

1. Open the workspace in the directory ${HOME}\jsf-security\ide\jdeveloper (use your favorite IDE).

2. Copy the com.groundside.jsf.securityresolver.adapter. J2EEContainerSecurityAttributeResolver class in the project core. Rename this copy as DatabaseSecurityAttributeResolver.

3. Modify the code as you see next:

```java
package com.groundside.jsf.securityresolver.adapter;

import java.util.Iterator;
import java.util.List;

import javax.faces.context.ExternalContext;
import javax.faces.context.FacesContext;

/**
 * Implementation of the security resolver that hooks into
 * J2EE Container Managed Security
 * @author Duncan Mills
 * $Id: J2EEContainerSecurityAttributeResolver.java,v 1.4
 * 2005/10/04 00:49:09 drmills Exp $
 */
/** This modified version provide roles stored in the database,
 * and the roles are added to the HttpSession context based on
 *user decision.
 */
public class DatabaseSecurityAttributeResolver extends
AbstractAttributeResolver{
    public DatabaseSecurityAttributeResolver() {
    }

    /**
     * Indicate the list of supported functions
```

```java
 * @param function to check for support as defined by a
 * constant in the <code>AttributeResolver</code>
 * @return true if this implementation supports this function
 */
public boolean isSupported(int function) {
    boolean supported = false;
    switch (function)  {
        case SECURED: {
                supported = true;
            }
        case AUTH_TYPE: {
                supported = true;
            }
            break;
        case PRINCIPAL_NAME: {
                supported = true;
            }
            break;
        case USER_IN_ROLE: {
                supported = true;
            }
            break;
        case USER_IN_ALL_ROLES: {
                supported = true;
            }
            break;
        default: {
                supported=false;
            }
            break;
    }
    return supported;
}

/**
 * Return a flag indicating if security is currently switched
 * on @param ctx FacesContext
 */
public boolean isSecurityEnabled(FacesContext ctx) {
    return (ctx.getExternalContext().getRemoteUser()!=null);
}
```

```java
/**
 * Get the remote user from the Faces External Context
 * @param ctx FacesContext
 * @return user name string
 */
public String getPrincipalName(FacesContext ctx) {
    return ctx.getExternalContext().getRemoteUser();
}


/**
 * Return the authorization type
 * @param ctx FacesContext
 */
public String getAuthenticationType(FacesContext ctx){
    return ctx.getExternalContext().getAuthType();
}

public boolean isUserInAllRoles(FacesContext ctx, List
roleDefinitions) {
    return matchUserRoles(ctx,roleDefinitions,true);
}

public boolean isUserInRole(FacesContext ctx, List
roleDefinitions) {
    return matchUserRoles(ctx,roleDefinitions,false);
}

/*
 * Internal function to check if the current user is in one
 * or all roles listed
 */
private boolean matchUserRoles(FacesContext fctx, List
roleDefinitions, boolean inclusive) {
    boolean authOk = false;
    ExternalContext ctx = fctx.getExternalContext();

    Iterator iter = roleDefinitions.iterator();

    List myRoles = (List) ctx.getSessionMap().get("myRoles");
```

```
        while (iter.hasNext())
          {
          String role = (String) iter.next();
          authOk = myRoles.contains(role);
          if ((inclusive && !authOk) || (!inclusive && authOk))
            {
             break;
            }
        }
        return authOk;
      }
    }
```

4. Open `com.groundside.jsf.securityresolver.Constants` source code and modify the `DEFAULT_SECURITY_RESOLVER` constant as following:

```
/**
  * The default resolver class
  */
public static final String DEFAULT_SECURITY_RESOLVER
= "com.groundside.jsf.securityresolver.adapter.
DatabaseSecurityAttributeResolver";
```

5. Next, repackage the project to get a new `jsf-security.jar` archive. Now the roles are added as an attribute to the `HttpSession` context (attribute is named `myRoles`).

How it works...

This time, roles are stored in a database, and they are added to the `HttpSession` context depending on choices made by the user in our application.

 Security constraints should be placed in your `web.xml`.

Using secured managed beans with JSF Security

As you know, J2EE allows you to protect web pages and other web resources such as files, directories, and servlets through declarative security. This approach won't provide protection to local beans. In this recipe, you will see how to extend JSF security configuration beyond web pages using managed bean methods. For this we will use the classes provided by Vinicius Senger on `http://blogs.sun.com/enterprisetechtips/entry/improving_jsf_security_configuration_with`.

Getting ready

Vinicius Senger has provided a sample application at `http://java.sun.com/mailers/techtips/enterprise/2007/download/ttsept2007FacesSec.zip`. This application contains all the classes necessary to secure local beans. Download this ZIP file and extract it to your favored location. You can try it with JSF 1.2 and 2.0.

How to do it...

Next, we will analyze Vinicius's solution and see how to use it. The two most important classes are the following (the sources of these classes are in the `/src` folder):

`br.com.globalcode.jsf.security.SecureActionListener`: This intercepts calls to managed bean methods and checks for annotated method permissions.

`br.com.globalcode.jsf.security.SecureNavigationHandler`: This forwards the user to a requested view if the user has the required credentials and roles.

These classes should be activated in your JSF descriptor, `faces-config.xml`, as shown:

```
<application>
  <action-listener>
    br.com.globalcode.jsf.security.SecureActionListener
  </action-listener>
  <navigation-handler>
    br.com.globalcode.jsf.security.SecureNavigationHandler
  </navigation-handler>
</application>
```

In addition, we can set up user object providers. You can choose between `ContainerUserProvider` and `SessionUserProvider`.

- `ContainerUserProvider`

The following is the context parameter to set up the default container user provider (since containers already provide declarative security, this configuration is all that you need):

```
<context-param>
  <param-name>jsf-security-user-provider</param-name>
  <param-value>
    br.com.globalcode.jsf.security.usersession.ContainerUserProvider
  </param-value>
</context-param>
```

`ContainerUserProvider` references the `ContainerUser` class. This class is available in the `\src\java\br\com\globalcode\jsf\security\container` folder.

- `SessionUserProvider`

In the case of a custom security authentication and authorization process, you can provide a user class adapter that implements the given user interface and bind a user object instance into the HTTP session with the key name `user`.

To begin with you have to create a `User` interface implementation. This interface provides two methods, named `getLoginName` and `isUserInRole` (in the package `model` there is a class `MyUser` representing a `User` implementation). Next you have to provide page login with a navigation case called `login` (this can be seen in the `login.jsp` page in the `/web` folder). And you must write a login managed bean that checks the user credentials and puts (or not) the user object into the HTTP session (in the `\src\java\controller` folder you can find the `LoginMB` example). Finally, you have to add a context parameter to the `web.xml` file to set up the user provider to look up the HTTP session for the `user` object:

```
<context-param>
  <param-name>jsf-security-user-provider</param-name>
  <param-value>
    br.com.globalcode.jsf.security.usersession.SessionUserProvider
  </param-value>
</context-param>
```

Vinicius has built an example of a JSF page that contains a `View` button and a `Delete` button (see the `index.jsp` page in the `/web` folder) and when the user press the `Delete` button then the `CustomerCRUD.delete` method called. This method includes an annotation that declares a required role for the method:

```
@SecurityRoles("customer-admin-adv, root")
    public String delete() {
      System.out.println("I'm a protected method!");
      return "delete-customer";
    }
```

The complete source code of `CustomerCRUD` is available in the `\src\java\controller` folder.

 You can test the sample application using the NetBeans IDE, since the application is packaged as a NetBeans project.

See also

The official page of this tip is at `http://blogs.sun.com/enterprisetechtips/entry/improving_jsf_security_configuration_with`. Thanks to Vinicius Senger for sharing this tip with us.

Using Acegi/Spring security in JSF applications

In this recipe, we will use Spring security support to develop a JSF login application. The big surprise is that we will not use the classical approach, which is very complicated and problematic.

Getting ready

We have developed this recipe with NetBeans 6.8, JSF 2.0, and GlassFish v3. The JSF 2.0 classes were obtained from the NetBeans JSF 2.0 bundled library. In addition, we have used Acegi/Spring libraries, which provide support for JSF 2.0. The necessary libraries are in the book code bundle, under the `/JSF_libs/Acegi-Spring – JSF 2.0` folder.

How to do it...

The key of this recipe consists in using an `HttpRequestDispatcher` to provide support for JSF and Spring Security to function properly (JSF first, Spring after it). The bean that will map login credentials and apply the `HttpRequestDispatcher` is listed next:

```
package packt.spring.login;

import java.io.IOException;

import javax.faces.context.ExternalContext;
import javax.faces.context.FacesContext;
import javax.servlet.RequestDispatcher;
import javax.servlet.ServletException;
import javax.servlet.ServletRequest;
```

```java
import javax.servlet.ServletResponse;

import org.springframework.context.annotation.Scope;
import org.springframework.stereotype.Component;

@Component
@Scope("request")
public class SpringLoginBean
{
  private String user;
  private String password;
  private boolean storeUser = false;
  private boolean logIn = false;

    public String getUser()
  {
    return this.user;
  }

  public void setUser(final String user)
  {
    this.user = user;
  }

  public String getPassword()
  {
    return this.password;
  }

  public void setPassword(final String password)
  {
    this.password = password;
  }

  public boolean isStoreUser()
  {
    return this.storeUser;
  }

  public void setStoreUser(final boolean storeUser)
  {
    this.storeUser = storeUser;
  }
  public boolean isLogIn()
  {
    return this.logIn;
  }

  public void setLogIn(final boolean logIn)
  {
```

```
    this.logIn = logIn;
  }

  public String loginAction() throws IOException, ServletException
  {
    ExternalContext context =
              FacesContext.getCurrentInstance().getExternalContext();
    RequestDispatcher dispatcher = ((ServletRequest)
                        context.getRequest()).getRequestDispatcher(
                                    "/j_spring_security_check");
    dispatcher.forward((ServletRequest) context.getRequest(),
    (ServletResponse) context.getResponse());
    FacesContext.getCurrentInstance().responseComplete();

    return null;
  }
}
```

[If you want you can also add a method to deal with bad credentials.]

Next, configure the Spring Security Filter Chain in web.xml to process Servlet FORWARD as
well as REQUEST.

```
<!-- Filter Config -->
<filter>
  <filter-name>springSecurityFilterChain</filter-name>
  <filter-class>
    org.springframework.web.filter.DelegatingFilterProxy
  </filter-class>
</filter>

<!-- Filter Mappings -->
<filter-mapping>
  <filter-name>springSecurityFilterChain</filter-name>
  <url-pattern>/*</url-pattern>
  <dispatcher>FORWARD</dispatcher>
  <dispatcher>REQUEST</dispatcher>
</filter-mapping>
```

The Spring Security configuration is accomplished in the `application_security-config.xml` file, listed next (the `login-processing-url` value is `/j_spring_security_check`, which is the location where the `HttpRequestDispatcher` will make the forward):

```xml
<?xml version="1.0" encoding="UTF-8"?>

<beans:beans
  xmlns="http://www.springframework.org/schema/security"
  xmlns:beans="http://www.springframework.org/schema/beans"
  xmlns:xsi="http://www.w3.org/2001/XMLSchema-instance"
  xsi:schemaLocation="http://www.springframework.org/schema/beans
  http://www.springframework.org/schema/beans/spring-beans-2.0.xsd
  http://www.springframework.org/schema/security
  http://www.springframework.org/schema/security/
  spring-security-2.0.1.xsd">
  <global-method-security
    secured-annotations="enabled">
  </global-method-security>

  <http auto-config="true"
    access-denied-page="/forbidden.jsp">

    <intercept-url
      pattern="/faces/secured**"
      access="ROLE_ADMIN,ROLE_GUEST" />
    <intercept-url
      pattern="/**"
      access="IS_AUTHENTICATED_ANONYMOUSLY" />

    <form-login
      login-processing-url="/j_spring_security_check"
      login-page="/faces/login.jsp"
      default-target-url="/"
      authentication-failure-url="/faces/login.jsp" />
    <logout
      logout-url="/logout*"
      logout-success-url="/" />

  </http>

  <!--
    User:admin  Password:admin
    User:guest  Password:guest
  -->
```

```
    <authentication-provider>
        <password-encoder hash="md5"/>
        <user-service>
            <user name="admin"
                  password="21232f297a57a5a743894a0e4a801fc3"
                  authorities="ROLE_ADMIN,ROLE_GUEST" />
            <user name="guest"
                  password="084e0343a0486ff05530df6c705c8bb4"
                  authorities="ROLE_GUEST" />
        </user-service>
    </authentication-provider>

</beans:beans>
```

Finally, the `login.jsp` page is in accordance with Spring Security's parameter naming specification. The submitted info is passed to the Spring Security Filter Chain (do not modify the `j_username`, `j_password`, `_spring_security_remember_me` IDs).

```
<%@page contentType="text/html" pageEncoding="UTF-8"%>

<%@taglib prefix="f" uri="http://java.sun.com/jsf/core"%>
<%@taglib prefix="h" uri="http://java.sun.com/jsf/html"%>

<!DOCTYPE HTML PUBLIC "-//W3C//DTD HTML 4.01 Transitional//EN"
    "http://www.w3.org/TR/html4/loose.dtd">

<f:view>
    <h:form id="loginForm" prependId="false">
        <h:panelGrid columns="4" footerClass="subtitle"
          headerClass="subtitlebig" styleClass="medium"
          columnClasses="subtitle,medium">
            <f:facet name="header">
                <h:outputText value="Login page:"/>
            </f:facet>
            <label for="j_username">
                <h:outputText value="User:" />
            </label>
            <h:inputText id="j_username" required="true" />

            <label for="j_password">
                <h:outputText value="Password:" />
            </label>
            <h:inputSecret id="j_password" required="true" />
```

```
                    <label for="_spring_security_remember_me">
                        <h:outputText value="Remember me" />
                    </label>
                    <h:selectBooleanCheckbox
                        id="_spring_security_remember_me" />
                    <h:outputText value=" "  />

                    <h:commandButton type="submit" id="login" action="#{spring
            LoginBean.loginAction}" value="Login" />
                </h:panelGrid>
            </h:form>

            <h:messages />
        </f:view>
```

The login page will look like the following screenshot (when the secured page is forbidden you will be forwarded to this page):

Login page:

User:	
Password:	
Remember me	☐
[Login]	

How it works...

Well, as you can see the idea is pretty simple. Instead of the hard work that is imposed by the classical approach, you can use a simple forward to a servlet. You don't even need a JSF backing bean, because the values only need to be intercepted by Spring Security on FORWARD. This is not a problem if you still want to take advantage of JSF converters and validations.

See also

The code bundled with this book contains a complete example of this recipe. The project can be opened with NetBeans 6.8 and it is named: `Acegi_Spring_security_in_JSF_ applications`.

Index

[PACKT] Thank you for buying
PUBLISHING
JSF 2.0 Cookbook: LITE

About Packt Publishing

Packt, pronounced 'packed', published its first book "*Mastering phpMyAdmin for Effective MySQL Management*" in April 2004 and subsequently continued to specialize in publishing highly focused books on specific technologies and solutions.

Our books and publications share the experiences of your fellow IT professionals in adapting and customizing today's systems, applications, and frameworks. Our solution based books give you the knowledge and power to customize the software and technologies you're using to get the job done. Packt books are more specific and less general than the IT books you have seen in the past. Our unique business model allows us to bring you more focused information, giving you more of what you need to know, and less of what you don't.

Packt is a modern, yet unique publishing company, which focuses on producing quality, cutting-edge books for communities of developers, administrators, and newbies alike. For more information, please visit our website: www.packtpub.com.

Writing for Packt

We welcome all inquiries from people who are interested in authoring. Book proposals should be sent to author@packtpub.com. If your book idea is still at an early stage and you would like to discuss it first before writing a formal book proposal, contact us; one of our commissioning editors will get in touch with you.

We're not just looking for published authors; if you have strong technical skills but no writing experience, our experienced editors can help you develop a writing career, or simply get some additional reward for your expertise.

Java EE 6 with GlassFish 3
Application Server

A practical guide to install and configure the GlassFish 3 Application Server and develop Java EE 6 applications to be deployed to this server

David Heffelfinger

Java EE 6 with GlassFish 3 Application Server

ISBN: 978-1-849510-36-3   Paperback: 488 pages

A practical guide to install and configure the GlassFish 3 Application Server and develop Java EE 6 applications to be deployed to this server

1. Install and configure the GlassFish 3 Application Server and develop Java EE 6 applications to be deployed to this server

2. Specialize in all major Java EE 6 APIs, including new additions to the specification such as CDI and JAX-RS

3. Use GlassFish v3 application server and gain enterprise reliability and performance with less complexity

GlassFish Security

Secure your GlassFish installation, Web applications, EJB applications, application client modules, and Web Services using Java EE and GlassFish security measures

Masoud Kalali

GlassFish Security

ISBN: 978-1-847199-38-6   Paperback: 296 pages

Secure your GlassFish installation, Web applications, EJB applications, Application Client modules, and Web services

1. Secure your GlassFish installation and J2EE applications

2. Develop secure Java EE applications including Web, EJB, and Application Client modules

3. Secure web services using GlassFish and OpenSSO web service security features

4. Support SSL in GlassFish including Mutual Authentication and Certificate Realm with this practical guide

Please check **www.PacktPub.com** for information on our titles

Spring Security 3

ISBN: 978-1-847199-74-4   Paperback: 396 pages

Secure your web applications against malicious intruders with this easy to follow practical guide

1. Make your web applications impenetrable

2. Implement authentication and authorization of users

3. Integrate Spring Security 3 with common external security providers

4. Packed full with concrete, simple, and concise examples

Java EE 5 Development with NetBeans 6

ISBN: 978-1-847195-46-3   Paperback: 400 pages

Develop professional enterprise Java EE applications quickly and easily with this popular IDE

1. Use features of the popular NetBeans IDE to improve Java EE development

2. Careful instructions and screenshots lead you through the options available

3. Covers the major Java EE APIs such as JSF, EJB 3 and JPA, and how to work with them in NetBeans

4. Covers the NetBeans Visual Web designer in detail

Please check **www.PacktPub.com** for information on our titles

CPSIA information can be obtained at www.ICGtesting.com
Printed in the USA
LVOW092302080512

280881LV00018B/3/P

9 781849 691628